For a New Critique of Political Economy

For a New Critique of Political Economy

BERNARD STIEGLER

translated by

Daniel Ross

polity

First published as *Pour une nouvelle critique de l'économie politique* © Éditions Galilée, 2009.

Économie de l'incurie et économie de la contribution © Bernard Stiegler, 2010.

This English edition © Polity Press, 2010

Ouvrage publié avec le concours du Ministère français de la Culture—Centre national du livre

Published with the assistance of the French Ministry of Culture—National Centre for the Book

Polity Press
65 Bridge Street
Cambridge CB2 1UR, UK

Polity Press
350 Main Street
Malden, MA 02148, USA

ISBN-13: 978-0-7456-4803-3 (hardback)
ISBN-13: 978-0-7456-4804-0 (paperback)

A catalogue record for this book is available from the British Library.

Typeset in 11 on 15 pt Adobe Garamond
by Servis Filmsetting Ltd, Stockport, Cheshire

The publisher has used its best endeavors to ensure that the URLs for external websites referred to in this book are correct and active at the time of going to press. However, the publisher has no responsibility for the websites and can make no guarantee that a site will remain live or that the content is or will remain appropriate.

Every effort has been made to trace all copyright holders, but if any have been inadvertently overlooked the publisher will be pleased to include any necessary credits in any subsequent reprint or edition.

For further information on Polity, visit our website: www.politybooks.com

CONTENTS

For a New Critique of Political Economy

For Arnauld de l'Épine and Christian Fauré

Heads buried in the sand: a warning

The theses put forward in this small volume were first set out on January 15, 2009 at the *Maison de l'Europe*, during a lecture which Évelyne Grossman and the *Collège international de philosophie* invited me to deliver, and they were also discussed in my contribution to the catalogue for "Work: Meaning and Care," an exhibition held in Dresden from June 2009 to March 2010 at the initiative of the Deutsches Hygiene-Museum, the German Federal Cultural Foundation and Daniel Tyradellis.

I decided to publish these reflections in the midst of economic and political debates taking place throughout the world about the necessity of implementing stimulus plans in order to limit the destructive effects of the first planetary economic crisis of the capitalist industrial world. Now when, in such debates, "investment stimulus" and "consumption stimulus" are spoken of in opposing terms, two distinct questions become confused, questions that, in fact, do require simultaneous treatment, yet according to two different scales of time, a difficulty which is all the greater, given that *the present crisis heralds the end of the consumerist model.*

Those who advocate stimulating consumption as the path to economic recovery want neither to hear nor speak about the end of consumerism. But the French government, which advocates stimulating investment, is no more willing than those who advocate stimulating consumption to call the consumerist industrial model into question. The French version of "stimulating investment" (which seems more subtle when it comes from Barack Obama) argues that the best way to save consumption is through investment, that is, by restoring "profitability," which will in turn restore an entrepreneurial dynamism itself founded upon consumerism and its counterpart, market-driven productivism.

In other words, this "investment"' proposes no long-term view capable of drawing any lessons from the collapse of an industrial model based on the automobile, on oil, and on the construction of highway networks, as well as on the Hertzien networks of the culture industries. This ensemble has until recently formed the basis of consumerism, yet today it is obsolete, a fact which became clear during the autumn of 2008. In other words, this "investment" is not an investment: it is on the contrary a *disinvestment,* an abdication which consists in doing no more than *burying one's head in the sand.*

4

This "investment policy," which has no goal other than the reconstitution of the consumerist model, is the translation of a moribund ideology, desperately trying to prolong the life of a model which has become self-destructive, denying and concealing for as long as possible the fact that the consumerist model is now massively toxic (a toxicity extending far beyond the question of "toxic assets") because it has reached its limits. This denial is a matter of trying, for as long as possible, to maintain the colossal profits that can be accrued by those capable of exploiting it.

The consumerist model has reached its limits because it has become systemically short-termist, because it has given rise to a *systemic stupidity* that *structurally prevents the reconstitution of a long-term horizon*. This "investment" is not an investment according to any terms other than those of pure accounting: it is a pure and simple reestablishment of the state of things, trying to rebuild the industrial landscape without at all changing its structure, still less its axioms, all in the hope of protecting income levels that had hitherto been achievable.

Such may be the hope, but these are the false hopes of those with buried heads. The genuine object of debate raised by the crisis, and by the question of how to escape this crisis, ought to be how to overcome the short-termism to which we have been led by a consumerism intrinsically destructive of all genuine investment—that is, of investment in the future—a short-termism which has *systemically, and not accidentally*, been translated into the *decomposition of investment into speculation*.

Whether we must, in order to avoid a major economic catastrophe, and to attenuate the social injustice caused by the crisis, stimulate consumption and the economic machine *such as it still is*, is a question as urgent as it is legitimate—as long as such a policy does not simply aggravate the situation at the cost of millions and billions of euros or dollars while at the same time masking the true question, which is to produce a vision and a political will capable of progressively *moving away from the economico-political complex of consumption* so as to *enter into the complex of a new type of investment*, which must be a social and political investment or, in other words, an investment in a common desire, that is, in what Aristotle called *philia*, and which would then form the basis of a new type of economic investment.

Between the absolute urgency which obviously imposes the imperative of salvaging the present situation—and of avoiding the passage from a global economic crisis to a global political crisis that might yet unleash military conflicts of global dimensions—and the absolute necessity that consists in producing a potential future in the form of a political and social will capable of making a break with the present situation, there is clearly a *contradiction*. Such a contradiction is characteristic of what happens to a dynamic system (in this case, the industrial system and the global capitalist system) once it has begun to *mutate*.

This question is political as much as it is economic: it is a question of political economy, a matter of *knowing in what precisely this mutation consists*, and to what political, but also industrial, choices it leads: it is a matter of *knowing what new industrial politics is required* (on this point at least, Barack Obama seems slightly ahead of the Europeans, who remain experts at functioning in a state of denial).

Only such a response is capable of simultaneously dealing with the question of what urgent and immediate steps are necessary in order to salvage the industrial system, and with the question of the how such steps must be inscribed within an economic and political mutation amounting to a revolution—if it is true that when a model has *run its course* [révolu], then its transformation, through which alone it can avoid total destruction, constitutes a *revolution*.

Introduction

Retentional economy

In 2001 I argued, in *La Technique et le Temps 3: Le temps du cinéma et la question du mal-être*, and by way of reading Kant's *Critique of Pure Reason,* for a *new critique*: for a critique addressing the question of tertiary retention, that is, the question of mnemotechnics—and in more general terms addressing the question of technics which, *qua materialization of experience*, always constitutes a *spatialization of the time of consciousness beyond consciousness* and, therefore, constitutes an unconsciousness, if not *the* unconscious. I would like to demonstrate here that this question of tertiary retention opens up a new perspective on political economy and its critique, and, now more than ever, that it makes a new critique of political economy the essential task of philosophy.

Conscious time is woven with what Husserl calls retentions and protentions.[1] Primary retention is that which is formed in the very passage of time, as the course of this time, such that, as a present which passes, it is

8

constituted by the immediate and primordial retention (the "primary retention") of its own passing. Becoming past, this passage of the present is then constituted as secondary retention, that is, as all those memorial contents [*souvenirs*] which together form the woven threads of our memory [*mémoire*].

Tertiary retention is a mnemotechnical exteriorization of secondary retentions which are themselves engendered by primary retentions. But from the beginning of that process of hominization that André Leroi-Gourhan describes as a process of exteriorization, all technical objects constitute an intergenerational support of memory which, as *material culture*, overdetermines learning [*apprentissages*] and mnesic activities. To this extent, therefore, tertiary retention always already precedes the constitution of primary and secondary retention. A newborn child arrives into a world in which tertiary retention both precedes and awaits it, and which, precisely, constitutes this world *as* world. And as the spatialization of individual time becoming thereby collective time, tertiary retention is an original exteriorization of the mind [*esprit*].

In the course of human history, however, the mnemotechnical retentional layer is transformed, increasing in both complexity and density. It leads in particular, from the advent of Neolithic sedentarization, to the formation of tertiary retention systems which constitute increasingly analytical recordings of primary and secondary retentional flows or fluxes [*flux*]—such as systems of writing and numeration. It is in this way that *logos* is constituted: as the discretization of the continuous flow of language which, spatialized, can then be considered analytically, which then enters into its diacritical era, and this is the point from which, fundamentally and specifically, logic proceeds. But this discretization of flows also affects gestures. The discretization of gesture was given concrete expression with the application of Jacques de Vaucanson's automation technology to the Jacquard loom, and became generalized in the form of the industrial revolution.

Gesture must here be considered (like speech) as a retentional flow, that is, as a *continuous chain* [*enchaînement*] of gestures, and the learning [*apprentissage*] of a craft consists in producing gestural secondary retentions, whereas the discretization and the spatialized reproduction of the time of gestures constitutes technical automation, but where it is no longer the *logos* of the *soul* but rather the gestures of the *body* that become *analytically reproducible* as tertiary retention. This reproducibility results in retentional grains that one can call *grammes*. And this is why we posit that the evolution of tertiary retention, from the Neolithic age until our own, constitutes a process of grammatization.

In the course of the nineteenth century, technologies for grammatizing *audiovisual perception* appear, through which the flows of the sensory organs are discretized. All noetic, psychomotor and aesthetic functions then find themselves transformed by grammatization processes. Considered in terms of political economy, this amounts to the fact that it is the functions of conception, production and consumption which are grammatized—and which are thereby incorporated into an apparatus devoted to the production of tertiary retentions controlled by *retentional systems*.[2]

The work of grammatization

I would like to show that:

- the question of tertiary retention, engendered as it is in the course of the process of grammatization, is the condition of the proletarianization described by Marx and Engels in the *Communist Manifesto*;
- new forms of grammatization, unknown to Marx and Engels, constitute new forms of proletarianization;
- from this perspective, a new critique of political economy is the task *par excellence* for philosophy.

This short book proposes a brief exposition of the considerations which constitute the basis of such a new critique of political economy, focused around several questions, in order to open a debate with Marx, and on the question of labor and work today—given that labor, which first appears with sedentarization, is always overdetermined by the state of grammatization which is current at the time, and given that grammatization is, at present, undergoing new and literally revolutionary developments.

The essential aspects of this exposition are the following:

- the *question of production*, at a moment when we are entering into a new economic and industrial era which, faced with the latest developments in grammatization, poses anew the question of the *definition* of labor;
- the *question of consumption*, and of what Marx was unable to foresee, which was the way in which consumption would be reconfigured in the twentieth century in an essential relation to desire and to its economy—in an essential relation to what, through the pathway to the imaginary, that is, to fantasy, and through that to the unconscious, transforms by binding to the material of the drives;

- the *question of the proletariat*, of the understanding and extension of this concept, of its uses and misuses in the Marxist tradition, of its being forgotten, and of its *immense importance today*;
- the *question of industry* and its inscription in human becoming, considered from the perspective of grammatization;
- the *question of externalities*, such as these are incessantly reconfigured in the course of the process of industrialization, insofar as industrialization is a process of grammatization, and in their relation to transindividuation, *that is, to commerce*;
- the question of *social classes* in the framework of a new proletarianization, of the disappearance of what one calls the bourgeoisie—petty, middle or grand—and the stakes of a becoming-mafia of capitalism.

Pharmacology of the proletariat

From commerce to the market

One hundred and fifty years ago, in January 1859, Marx published his *Contribution to a New Critique of Political Economy*, and hence when I argue here for a new critique of political economy, I am also commemorating this anniversary. But, at the same time, I am paying homage to the journal, *La Nouvelle Critique*, about which I spoke in September 2008 at an annual event sponsored by the newspaper *L'Humanité*,[1] describing the place this journal holds in my personal history as an adolescent and young militant: it was in the pages of this Communist Party publication that for the first time I read about psychoanalysis, linguistics, anthropology and philosophy.

Finally, and above all, in speaking *today* about a new *critique*, I am engaging in polemical dialogue with an intellectual tradition which is very much my own, emerging from French philosophy in the second half of the twentieth century, and which, as post-

14

structuralism—following Barthes, author of *Critical Essays*, and about whom I also heard for the first time in *La Nouvelle Critique*—posited that critique was a concept inseparable from metaphysics, that it was to this extent itself metaphysical, and that, henceforth, it would be less a matter of "critiquing" than of deconstructing.

In my own view, deconstruction remains a critique, and it is as such that it remains invaluable. But none of this is very clear, and I would say that, in a way, deconstruction failed to critique its critique of critique, failed, that is, to critique the claim that the form taken by critique has historically been metaphysical. In other words, it has not clarified what a critique might be *were it no longer founded on a system of oppositions.*

What do I mean when I speak of having to *start afresh* in the critique of political economy? And first of all, what is political economy? I will not in fact give any kind of detailed answer to this question, which has in any case already been meticulously explored by Gido Berns. I will restrict myself to pointing out that, whereas Berns relates the definition of political economy given by Antoine de Montchrestien in 1615 (according to which it refers to an economy surpassing the domestic sphere of the *oikos*) to the question of *commerce* formulated by Arnould in 1791, in this work here it is a matter of a political economy *which is no longer strictly commercial*, if it is true that *commerce* is a type of exchange irreducible to what happens to the *market* when industrialization and mechanization create new forms of exchange.

Commerce is always an exchange of *savoir-faire* [knowledge of how to make or do] and *savoir-vivre* [knowledge of how to live]. It is in this same sense, furthermore, that "commerce" may, in French, refer to conversation and more generally to all forms of fruitful social relation. On the other hand, however, the *consumerist* market presupposes the liquidation of both *savoir-faire* and *savoir-vivre*. (The difference between commerce and the market was recently affirmed and explored by Franck Aggeri, Olivier Favereau and Armand Hatchuel at a colloquium in Cerisy-la-Salle, "*L'activité marchande sans le marché?*")[2]

Philosophers, economy, and ideology today

In the spring of 2008, Évelyne Grossman invited me to speak at the *Collège international de philosophie*, and I suggested speaking on the theme which forms the title of the present work, because I was convinced that we were on the verge of an unprecedented crisis, a crisis calling *as such* for a *new* critique of political economy—

the specifics of which I analyze in greater detail in *Pour en finir avec la mécroissance: Quelques propositions d'Ars Industrialis*.[3]

There was also, however, another reason for speaking about this subject: I wanted to provoke a discussion within contemporary philosophy about the state of its political discourse, given that so often, if not indeed most of the time, French philosophers from my own and the preceding generation have (with some notable exceptions)[4] *nothing* whatsoever to say about the contemporary economy, as if nothing new had appeared in this domain since the end of the Second World War; or, again, as if there were a prohibition on any philosophical intervention in the field of economics after the advent of "economism"—the economism of the infamous "homo economicus," since become shameful—an economism which encompasses Marxism (liquidating "the political"), leading to all those terrible mistakes of which we are now aware.

I will try here, then, to open up a conversation with those who come to us from this twentieth century. But I would also and above all like to invite their readers, and among the latter, those who, unlike myself, are still young philosophers, and those who are not employed as philosophers, but who study philosophy because they have made it their *otium*: all those who are not professional philosophers, but who are lovers [*amateurs*] of philosophy and, as such, friends of wisdom—that is, who are, as such, true philosophers.

In opening up this exchange, what I want to say before anything else is the following: the philosophy of our time has abandoned the project of a critique of political economy, and this constitutes a disastrous turn of events. Because if it is true that economism has led to horrific outcomes, nevertheless the absence of a critique of today's economy prepares other horrors—and at the same time leaves the coming generation tragically unprepared. As for this philosophical abdication in relation to economics—which characterizes the attitudes of so many and which amounts to a renunciation of the attempt to think their time, and which is as such a correlate of the renunciation by politicians of the notion of struggling against a state of things which undermines the law—this abdication was brought about by a certain relation to critique, or rather by a non-relation, such that it leads to a non-relation to current economics— often masked by an obsessive relation to philosophical texts devoted to the economics of the past.

Now, this non-relation, which has become an occlusion if not indeed an outright denial, was *also* produced, in large part, by the *same processes* that led financiers, industrialists, technocrats and politicians to *interior-*

ize certain situations as simply given, whereas they are in reality unsustainable artifices: they will, inevitably, reach their limits, and it will then become necessary to submit these limits to a critique, in the Kantian sense of this word. These processes form what used to be called "*ideology*." This ideology is beginning to reappear, this time *as such*: it is beginning to appear for what it is, thanks to a very brutal revelation of these limits. And yet, when faced with such questions, philosophy remains almost entirely mute.

To think and to critique political economy as *commerce* that has become *exchange* under the conditions of an industrial society—that is, that has submitted to a *mutation of labor*, to a functionalization of the processes of production and consumption, to a resultant *functionalization of social relations*, and such that they can no longer be envisaged without mechanical technology—requires aiming at the examination of both economics and politics, and speaking about them insofar as they are indissociable.[5]

As for the political discourse of French philosophers, they say practically nothing about economics. They speak of immigration, of Europe, or of democracy, but they do not speak of capital, nor labor, nor industry, nor marketing. As for those who do speak philosophically about work and labor—and there are a few—they are both interesting and important, but they are in general not philosophers: they are sociologists or economists, or even computer scientists.

The question of work

Faced with increases in productivity gains due to automation and digitalization, and with the unemployment to which this gave rise, a major debate took place at the end of the twentieth century on the possibility and necessity of shared work. It was in this context that in France, the government of Lionel Jospin, under the authority of Minister of Social Affairs Martine Aubry, passed a law limiting the working week to thirty-five hours.

This law was inspired by research published in 1995, both by Jeremy Rifkin in the United States (the French translation of this work was prefaced by Michel Rocard)[6] and by Dominique Méda in France,[7] influenced in turn by the research of André Gorz, in particular his work, *Métamorphoses du travail: Critique de la raison économique.*[8] More recently, after the election of Jacques Chirac in 2002, questions were raised, in the first place by the Minister of Culture Jean-Jacques Aillagon, about the role of Unédic (the French unemployment welfare

20

agency), and about the laws determining the conditions under which occasional and casual workers in the theatre and cinema [*intermittents du spectacle*] could qualify for unemployment benefits. This in turn led Antonella Corsani and Maurizio Lazzarato again to address the question of work.[9]

During this same period, new work practices appeared in the wake of digital and reticulated technologies, with respect to which innovative discourses developed in France and elsewhere, discourses which invite us to revisit the definition of work in its relation to what I describe as a *pharmakon*—and as an hypomnesic *pharmakon*, that is, as a *technology of the spirit* which, as tertiary retention, can just as well lead to the proletarianization of the life of the mind as it can to its critical intensification, when it finds itself confronted with what McKenzie Wark calls "abstraction."[10] These new work practices have brought profoundly into question the way in which work is distributed in the productivist and consumerist industrial epochs, questions which have frequently been raised by the journal *Multitudes*, and by the director of this journal, Yann Moulier-Boutang, opening the question of an economy of contribution and reinvigorating the question of property.

It was in this context that an important proposal resurfaced, from Rifkin to Lazzarato, a proposal first suggested by Milton Friedman, and one that, when it recurs during the global crisis, does so with renewed force: the idea of implementing a negative tax allowing the remuneration of non-salaried work. Corsani and Lazzarato, furthermore, show that the benefits regime in place for French occasional and casual theatrical and cinematic workers is a case of just such a negative taxation system.

But with this proposition, just as with all those new work practices invented by those whom Pekka Himanem[11] and McKenzie Wark call "hackers," the question of *work time outside of employment* is posed with renewed vigour, having been totally ignored by the law reducing the working week to thirty-five hours, just as it ignored the exhaustion of the consumerist industrial model, a model within which production and consumption constitute a functional opposition, but one that has now become obsolete.[12]

Today, as we undergo a global economic crisis of unusual violence, one that seems to constitute the end of a long cycle that is at once industrial and economic,[13] can we keep posing the question of work in the same terms? Does the shake-up of the consumerist model that has taken place not profoundly alter the stakes and even the definition of work, given that the latter was essentially conceived, over the preceding century, in accordance with an industrial model resting on the coupling of production and consumption, and given that it is precisely this functional pair that now seems to have exhausted itself?[14] This is precisely the question raised by the research of Corsani and Lazzarato, considered from the standpoint of the current crisis and of its destructive effects on the classical forms of work.

1908–2008: *The tendential fall of the rate of profit and the consumerist response*

The industrial capitalism of the productivist nineteenth century, founded on the steam engine and on the iron rails of railway networks, gives way in the twentieth century to a consumerist model founded on the steel industry, the petrochemical industry, and on road networks. One hundred and fifty years after the *Contribution to a Critique of Political Economy*, however, the productivist and consumerist industrial model, having become global, has in fact *disintegrated, and has done so* to the precise extent that it has consisted in the economic and functional integration of production and consumption.

If in 1908, with the launch of the Model T, Henry Ford invented a new industrial model which appeared to counter the effects of the tendency of the rate of profit to fall,[15] nevertheless in the course of 2008 the Ford Motor Company managed to lose three quarters of its value—while at the same time the road networks of carbon-time and mobility founded on the consumption of hydrocarbons are being replaced by digital networks of light-time and the development of an economy of the hypermaterial.[16] These questions have received detailed analysis in *Pour en finir avec la mécroissance*.[17]

It is in this context of light-time (dominated by the issues of access to electronic networks and of digital automation) that Jeremy Rifkin proposes the following hypothesis:

> Perhaps as little as 5 percent of the adult population will be needed to manage and operate the traditional industrial sphere by the year 2050.[18]

Why is it that Rifkin and others who reflect on the question of work fail to analyze the relation between what they call the "end of work" and the tendential fall in the rate of profit, and why is it that, after 1968 and above all after the 1980s (that is, after the "conservative revolution"), it was so frequently proclaimed that Marx was mistaken when he formulated this thesis?

Marx and Engels predicted that capitalism, or what

one calls the market economy, would rapidly reach its limit as the role of labor—that is, variable capital—diminishes due to productivity gains achieved in the global economy of production. Now, those concerned in the 1990s with the question of work agreed that productivity gains would inevitably lead to an "end of work," but seemed also to share the idea, widely held in the wake of the "conservative revolution" and the ideological domination of neo-liberalism, that the capitalist dynamic had *overcome* the tendential fall in the rate of profit.

Nothing could be more false, and Marx was in fact far from mistaken. The recent crisis is, very simply put, a consequence of this *systemic* tendency. Marx could not, however, have anticipated the role of the exploitation and functionalization of a *new energy*, which is not the energy of the proletarianized producer (labor as pure labor force), nor the motor energy of a new industrial apparatus (such as oil and electricity, which are placed into the service of the steel industry and the culture industries), but rather the energy of the *proletarianized consumer*—that is, the consumer's *libidinal* energy, the exploitation of which changes the libidinal *economy* and, with it, the economy *as a whole*, to the point where the former is destroyed just like the latter, and the former *by* the latter.

In other words, Marx was unable to anticipate the way in which the question of consumption arises in the twentieth century, and the way in which this transforms the landscape which Marx tried to describe in *Capital*. Marx did, of course, address the issue of consumption, and he did so frequently. Consider, for example, the following passage from *Contribution to the Critique of Political Economy* (1859):

> Consumption is simultaneously also production, just as in nature the production of a plant involves the consumption of elemental forces and chemical materials. [. . .] But the same applies to any other kind of consumption which [. . .] contributes to the production of some aspect of man. Nevertheless, says political economy, this type of production that is identical with consumption is a second phase arising from the destruction of the first product. In the first type of production the producer assumes an objective aspect, in the second type the objects created by him assume a personal aspect.[19]

And especially:

> Hunger is hunger; but the hunger that is satisfied by cooked meat eaten with fork and knife differs from hunger that devours raw meat [. . .] Production thus produces

not only the object of consumption but also the mode of consumption.[20]

Marx here underlines in a certain way the question of *relations of consumption*—which poses the question of what I will describe in what follows as *processes of transindividuation.*

And yet, this question of consumption will not enable him to think the *new form of proletarianization* consisting in the organization of *consumption as the destruction of savoir-vivre with the aim of creating available purchasing power*, thereby refining and reinforcing that system which rested on the *destruction of savoir-faire with the aim of creating available labor force*. It does not enable him, in other words, to anticipate what, in the twentieth century, in the form of the capitalist libidinal economy, will make possible the *deferral of but also the aggravation of the effects of, the tendential fall in the rate of profit.*

This is the very question posed by Guy Debord, who extends the concept of proletarianization— as the expropriation of human time submitted to commodity-time—to the figure of the consumer.[21] Debord was unable, however, to connect this change in the capitalist system to the *pharmacological* question of the exteriorization techniques discussed below.

It is only possible to come to grips with this question by way of Freud and the uses which marketing made of his theory of the unconscious—in particular those instigated by his nephew, Edward Bernays, who played an essential role in the history of American capitalism, as shown by Adam Curtis in his 2002 documentary, *The Century of the Self*. Before returning to this point—which has been utterly neglected by those concerned with the question of work, in spite of the fact that productivism and consumerism are inseparable—we must first proceed more profoundly into the question of the essence of that process of proletarianization through which, according to Marx and Engels, labor undergoes radical change, but a process which is also, in my opinion, the condition of possibility of consumerism insofar as this entails the proletarianization of the consumer.

Now, as surprising as it may seem, it is necessary at this point to return to the very origin of philosophy, and to its struggle against sophistry, in order to propose that the first thinker of the proletariat, who thinks the proletariat without knowing that he does so, if I may put it this way, but who thereby grants *us* the possibility of thinking the proletariat, is Plato.

Plato and the proletariat

Jacques Derrida, in "Plato's Pharmacy,"[22] developed a large part of his project of the deconstruction of metaphysics on the basis of his reading of *Phaedrus*, by showing how this dialogue opposes philosophical *anamnesis* (that is, the remembrance of the truth of being) to sophistic *hypomnesis* (that is, to mnemotechnics, and in particular to writing as a fabricator of illusion and a technique for the manipulation of minds), and by showing that it is *impossible*—according to what Derrida describes in *Of Grammatology* as a *logic* of that supplement which is the trace—to *oppose* the interior (*anamnesis*) and the exterior (*hypomnesis*): it is impossible to oppose *living* memory to the *dead* memory of the *hypomnematon*, which the final Foucault will find so interesting and which *constitutes* living memory as learned [*savante*]. This impossibility opens the *pharmacological question*, according to which the hypomnesic is a *pharmakon*: at once poison and remedy.

Now, what Socrates describes in *Phaedrus*, namely that the *exteriorization of memory is a loss of memory and knowledge*, has today become the stuff of everyday experience in *all* aspects of our existence, and, more and more often, in the feeling of our powerlessness [*impuissance*], if not of our *impotence* [impotence], indeed of

29

our *obsolescence*—at the very moment when the extraordinary *mnesic power* of digital networks makes us aware of the immensity of human memory, which appears to have become infinitely recoverable and accessible.

The spread of industrial hypomnesic apparatuses causes our memories to pass into machines, in such a way that, for example, we no longer know the telephone numbers of those close to us—while the spread of spell checkers causes fear of the end of *orthographic consciousness* and of the literary hypomnesic knowledge that goes with it and, *with that*, the anamnesic knowledge of language.

Now, this amounts to the everyday and perceptible aspect of what I would like to present here as a vast process of *cognitive and affective proletarianization*—and a vast process of the loss of knowledge(s): *savoir-faire, savoir-vivre*, theoretical knowledge [*savoir théoriser*], *in the absence of which all savor is lost.*

When *exteriorization*, which plays a major role in *The German Ideology*, and which is the root of the technical question, that is, the question of this production of self by self in which the human consists, reaches the stage where the exteriorization of memory and knowledge becomes hyperindustrial, then it is at once what extends without limit the power of *hypomnesic milieus*, and what allows them to be controlled—controlled by the *cognitive and cultural industries* of control socie-ties which now formalize neurochemical activity and nucleotide sequences, and which thereby inscribe the neurobiological substrates of memory and knowledge into the history of what one must analyze as a *process of grammatization* (that is, of discretization, and as such of abstraction from a continuum), a history the most recent stage of which is that of biotechnologies, and the *next* stage of which is nanotechnologies. Hence arises the question of a biopolitical, psychopolitical, sociopo-litical, and technopolitical industrial economy, and, in the final analysis, of a *noopolitical* industrial economy of memory.

It is with the advent of mnemotechnics that the process of exteriorization qua technical becoming expressly becomes a history of grammatization. The process of grammatization is the *technical history of memory*, in which hypomnesic memory continually reintroduces the constitution of a *tension* within anam-nesic memory. This anamnesic tension is exteriorized in the form of works of the mind [or of the spirit, *esprit*], through which epochs of psychosocial *individuation and disindividuation* are pharmacologically configured.

Grammatization is the process through which the flows and continuities which weave our existences are *discretized*: writing, as the discretization of the flow of speech, is a *stage* of grammatization. And grammatization occurs within an organology the question of which is introduced in *Anti-Oedipus*:

> The primitive territorial machine codes flows, invests organs, and marks bodies. [. . .] [T]he man who enjoys the full exercise of his rights and duties has his whole body marked under a régime that consigns his organs and their exercise to the collectivity [. . .]. For it is a founding act—that the organs be hewn into the socius, and that the flows run over its surface—through which man ceases to be a biological organism and becomes a full body, an earth, to which his organs become attached, where they are attracted, repelled, miraculated, following the requirements of a socius. Nietzsche says: it is a matter of creating a memory for man; and man, who was constituted by means of an active faculty of forgetting (*oubli*), by means of a repression of biological memory, must create an *other* memory, one that is collective [. . .]. "Perhaps indeed there was nothing more fearful and uncanny in the whole prehistory of man than his *mnemotechnics*."[23]

Now, with the industrial revolution, the process of grammatization constituting the history of mnemotechnics *suddenly surpasses the sphere of language*, that is, also, the sphere of *logos*, with which it is placed by Deleuze

32

and Guattari in an essential and original relation:[24] the process of grammatization invests bodies. And in the first place, it discretizes the *gestures* of producers with the aim of making possible their *automatic reproduction*—while at the very same moment there also appear those machines and apparatuses for reproducing the visible and the audible that so caught the attention of Walter Benjamin, machines and apparatuses which grammatized perception and, through that, the affective activity of the nervous system.

The grammatization of gesture, which was the basis of what Marx described as proletarianization, that is, as *loss of savoir-faire*, is then pursued with the development of electronic and digital devices to the point that *all* forms of knowledge become grammatized via cognitive and cultural mnemotechnologies. This will include the way in which linguistic knowledge becomes the technologies and industries of automated language processing, but it will also include *savoir-vivre*, that is, behavior in general, from user profiling to the grammatization of affects—all of which will lead toward the "cognitive" and "cultural" capitalism of the hyperindustrial *service* economies.

Grammatization is the history of the exteriorization of memory in all its forms: nervous and cerebral memory, corporeal and muscular memory, biogenetic memory. When technologically exteriorized, memory can become the object of sociopolitical and biopolitical controls through the economic investments of social organizations, which thereby *rearrange psychic organizations* through the intermediary of mnemotechnical organs, among which must be counted machine-tools (Adam Smith analyzed as early as 1776 the effects of the machine on the mind of the worker) and all automata—including household appliances, as well as the "internet of things" and the communicating devices that would soon invade the hyperindustrial market, and which are *hypomnesic objects* through which what Scott Lash and Celia Lury have described as *thingification*[25] takes a new turn.[26]

This is why the thinking of grammatization calls for a *general organology*, that is, a theory of the articulation of bodily organs (brain, hand, eyes, touch, tongue, genital organs, viscera, neuro-vegetative system, etc.), artificial organs (tools, instruments and technical supports of grammatization) and social organs (human groupings, such as families, clans, or ethnicities, political institutions and societies, businesses and economic organizations, international organizations, and social systems in general, regardless of the extent to which they are or are not deterritorialized, and whether they be juridical, linguistic, religious, political, fiscal, economic, etc.).[27]

If in the hyperindustrial era we reopen the question posed in *Phaedrus* concerning the hypomnesic object, and if we do so from the standpoint of this kind of general organology (founding a *political organology*, an *economic organology*, and an *aesthetic organology*), we discover that the Platonic question of hypomnesis constitutes the first version of a thinking of proletarianization, insofar as it is true that the proletariat are those economic actors who are without knowledge because they are without memory: their memory has passed into the machine that reproduces gestures that the proletariat no longer needs to know – they must simply serve the reproductive machine and thus, once again, they become serfs.

Examining the question of technical memory today means *reopening the question of hypomnesis not only as the question of the proletariat*, but also as a process of grammatization in which it is *consumers who are henceforth deprived of memory and knowledge by the service industries and their apparatuses*. We shall see how this produces short-circuits in the transindividuation process. Examining the question of technical memory today means investigating the stage of *generalized proletarianization* induced by the spread of hypomnesic technologies.

The truth of Plato would then be found in Marx, but

only on the condition that two supplementary conclusions are drawn:

- Marx himself fails to think the hypomnesic character of technics and human existence, which accounts for the fact that he is unable to think human life as *ex*-istence and hence for the fact that, like Plato, he continues to *oppose* the dead and the living.
- The *inaugural* struggle of philosophy against sophistic around this question of memory and its technicization is the heart of that political struggle which philosophy was from the very beginning. Hence the reevaluation of the place of hypomnesis in Plato, as well as the deconstruction of the Platonic account of hypomnesis which Derrida proposed, must constitute the basis of a renewed project of a critique of political economy by philosophy, a critique *in which technics becomes the central stake*, and in which is posed the threefold question of an organology, a pharmacology and a therapeutic—it is therefore the question of a sociotherapy,[28] which is what political economy is, and of which grammatization is the dynamic process.

Proletarianization as loss of knowledge

The proletarian, we read in Gilbert Simondon, is a *disindividuated* worker, a laborer whose knowledge has passed into the machine in such a way that it is no longer the worker who is individuated through bearing tools and putting them into practice. Rather, the laborer serves the machine-tool, and it is the latter that has become the technical individual—in the sense that it is within the machine-tool, and within the technical system to which it belongs, that an individuation is produced. This technical individuation is, according to Simondon, a process of concretization through which the system of industrial objects becomes functionally integrated and thereby transformed—as does the sociotechnical milieu. The proletarianized laborer, however, is literally excluded from this transformation—*dissociated* from it, not *associated* with it. Such a laborer is not co-individuated. He does not ex-ist.

This dissociation is in reality a rupture in the *transindividual fabric which constitutes the labor environment*, as it does all *symbolic* milieus, given that work is clearly *also* one such symbolic milieu. In the milieu of associated work, the workers, through their work, fashion an experience in which they cause their milieu to evolve—their tools, for example, or the way in which they are used, not to mention, of course, the products of their use. They *open up* [*ouvrent*] this milieu of which they are the workers [*ouvriers*]. Proletarianization is that which excludes this participation of the producer from the evolution of the conditions of production, and through which he works.

In other words, proletarianization is a process of losing knowledge—that is, also, a loss of savor and of existence—which is engendered by grammatization insofar as it short-circuits the processes of transindividuation through which, by becoming individuated through work, that is, though learning something, the worker individuates the milieu of their work. It is just such a short-circuit which constitutes the stakes of that loss of knowledge by which Marx and Engels defined proletarianization in the *Communist Manifesto* of 1848:

> The less the skill and exertion of strength implied in manual labor, in other words, the more modern industry becomes developed, the more is the labor of men superseded by that of women. Differences of age and sex have no longer any distinctive social validity for the working class. All are instruments of labor, more or less expensive to use, according to their age and sex.[29]

This expense is what Marx and Engels call labor power, which is, then, no longer a knowledge but becomes instead a commodity. From a bearer of tools and a practitioner of instruments, the worker has himself become a tool and an instrument in the service of a tool-bearing machine. Now, as was precisely indicated by Marx and Engels, this is the fate of *all* producers, and not only of workers:

> The lower strata of the middle class—the small trades-people, shopkeepers, and retired tradesmen generally, the handicraftsmen and peasants—all these sink gradually into the proletariat [. . .]. Thus the proletariat is recruited from all classes of the population.[30]

Certainly, in the *Manifesto* as in the *Contribution*, the *Grundrisse* and in *Capital,* the proletariat is always presented as being comprised precisely of the working class. But that this is so is due to a state of historical fact, tied to an *archaic* stage (archaic in all senses of the term) of the development of capitalism and industry, *that is, of grammatization*, and which is destined to evolve appreciably by bringing into the process of proletarianization all those whose knowledge is absorbed by hypomnesic processes consisting not only in machines, but in apparatuses, expert systems, services, networks, and technological objects and systems of all kinds.

Proletarianization and pharmacology

The proletariat is not the working class. All of Marxism has misinterpreted Marx in confusing the two. A typical case can be found, for example, in Jacques Rancière's *The Nights of Labor: The Workers' Dream in 19th Century France*.[31] But on the other hand, and above all, grammatization, by allowing the harnessing [*captation*] of the attention of consumers and, through that, the harnessing of their libidinal energy, made equally possible their proletarianization, by destroying their *savoir-vivre*, and not only their *savoir-faire*. This proletarianization of consumers is what made it possible—by opening up mass markets enabling resistance against the tendential fall of the rate of profit—to confer *buying power* upon consumers, to accord them *more* than simply the renewal of their *labor power*, and to fundamentally and *practically* weaken the Marxist theory of class struggle.

The problem is that the surplus that has by necessity been redistributed to proletarianized producers who have become consumers led, toward the end of the twentieth century, to the destruction of their libidinal energy and to its decomposition into drives—the result of what Herbert Marcuse called "desublimation." We must therefore engage in a critique of libidinal economy: *a new critique of political economy is necessary, and it must also constitute a pharmacological critique of libidinal economy.*

Freudian theory will only allow these questions to be advanced to the extent that it, too, is confronted with the question of the *pharmakon* that is the fetish, and with the question of grammatization such as it transforms fetishism—which takes place through an analysis of the role of *hypomnemata*[32] in the history of desire and sublimation, the transitional object being a kind of proto-*hypomnematon* and proto-fetish,[33] while contemporary hypomnesic objects are *hypomnemata* that henceforth link networks together.

The proletarianization of the consumer is an epoch of libidinal economy, and a crucial task of the new critique of political economy is to construct a *genealogy* of this economy, which is a pharmacology the genesis of which is indissociable from organological becoming and grammatization. Now, this pharmacology raises the question of *transindividuation* insofar as it *can produce long circuits of individuation as well as short-circuits*, that is, *disindividuations*.

What Plato calls *anamnesis* is hence founded on a dialectic, and this is a *dia-logical commerce* through which, in interlocution, that is, in a "dialogism" that I also understand in Bakhtin's sense of the term,[34] long circuits of transindividuation are formed, which tend

41

to be short-circuited by the poisonous uses to which the sophists put this literal *pharmakon*.

More generally, if the grammatization of perception and of the nervous system—insofar as it is the seat of the affects—can lead to the proletarianization of consumers, that is, destroy their *savoir-vivre*, as well as the savors which these arts of living can procure, this is because libidinal economy in general constitutes circuits of desire within a process of transindividuation through which libidinal energy is formed and accumulated, but this is also a process in which grammatization may either:

- create long circuits, that is, *accumulate libidinal energy by intensifying individuation*, and give objects of desire to the individual that infinitize his or her individuation (Simondon shows that individuation is structurally unachievable and in this sense infinite), because these objects can only be given *as* infinite and incommensurable; or
- provoke short-circuits, that is, disindividuation, and consequently desublimation, that is, the *commensurable finitization of all things*, leading to the destruction of libidinal energy.

Grammatization is *irreducibly* pharmacological, and *hypomnemata* can therefore either:

- proletarianize the *psyche* which it affects; or
- individuate this *psyche* by inscribing it within the *new* circuit of transindividuation that it connects up, and through which long circuits are formed, tied to what Plato apprehended as an *anamnesis*—which is a circuit giving access to a truth founded on the projection of an idea, that is, of a consistence: of an object which does not exist, because it does not have any foundation in the subsistences which constitute the order of the commensurable, but which is *the very object of desire insofar as it consists incommensurably.*

It is this type of circuit grounding a commerce that the short-circuit replaces, through a market on which nothing remains except commensurabilities (for example, labor power without *savoir-faire*, forming a buying power without *savoir-vivre*)—this is a *market of fools* [dupes]. For in the final analysis, this market is not a market. And this is something which Socrates already noted, contra Gorgias.

Nevertheless, an economy of *pharmaka* is a therapeutic that does not result in a hypostasis opposing poison and remedy: the economy of the *pharmakon* is a *composition* of tendencies, and not a dialectical struggle between *opposites*.[35] The concrete expression of this composition consists in arrangements of the three levels of general organology, such that these constitute a *system of care*: individuation at the pharmacological level (technical individuation) transductively intensifies the individuation of the other two levels (psychic individuation and collective individuation).

On the other hand, a *dis-economy*[36] of *pharmaka* is what results from the appearance of any new *pharmakon* insofar as it short-circuits the other two levels—and this is occurring today with the technologies of "social networking,"[37] for which no political economy and no system of care is prescribed by any public authority; or, again, it is what occurs in the course of the synaptogenesis of the infantile cerebral organ when the audiovisual short-circuits the transitional object, the infantile psychic apparatus being thereby proletarianized.[38]

FOUR

To work

The proletarianization of the nervous system, systemic stupidity, and new commerce

The more the place of producers shrinks, the more must markets and the number of consumers be enlarged, automation ceaselessly widening the field of proletarianization while diminishing the role of labor—that is, of variable capital. *Trading* has itself been automated. Engineers have themselves been proletarianized. The engineer who conceived, developed, installed, and managed a system has disappeared. Today there are "processes," where more and more *hypomnemata* intervene to short-circuit psychic individuals at every level.

Within these processes, it is the labor power of the nervous system that is being ever more proletarianized, and the *proletarians of the nervous system* are no less deprived of knowledge than are the *proletarians of the muscular system*. The knowledge of which they have been stripped, however, is not that of *savoir-faire*: it is *theoretical* knowledge—that is, knowledge which is noetic in actuality. A psychopower then develops that controls consumers (in which case it is a matter of channeling the libido) as well as producers *and designers*, whose nervous energy must be placed into the service of "technical ensembles," as Simondon calls them.

We thus have *pure cognitive labor power utterly devoid of knowledge*: with cognitive technologies, it is the cognitive itself which has been proletarianized.[1] In this consists, then, cognitive capitalism, also known as "creative" or "immaterial" capitalism. And this is concretely expressed in the fact that *the cognitive has been reduced to calculability—logos* has become, pharmacologically and economically, *ratio*.[2]

If skilled professions [*métiers*] do in fact still remain, very few are connected with that type of production that is called "creative," and most of the time such jobs are not really creative. For to be creative—that is, to *work* [*oeuvrer*—to work on something, to open up a work]—is to produce negentropy. But those who are called "creative workers" today are in fact merely creators of that kind of "value" which is *capable of being evaluated on the market*, like press officers or public relations officials who work toward the *entropic adaptation* of the system, but who do not create any works or open up any work [*mais qui n'oeuvrent à rien du tout*]: to work [*oeuvrer*] always means to work *with the incalculable*—that is, to work with that infinity of the desirable which means that a process of individuation is constituted *through its unachievability*.

Such is the reality of what Maurizio Lazzarato calls "the cooperation between brains,"[3] as it is produced through grammatization systems which make possible the proletarianization of all those tasks conducted at the highest levels of nervous system activity. This results in the formation of a *systemic stupidity*, making possible among other things Alan Greenspan's attempt to explain before the House of Representatives how he could in all sincerity have led the world to the brink of catastrophe, as well as the cretinization of those "financial elites" who discovered they'd been rolled by Bernard Madoff: the elites have themselves been proletarianized, that is, *deprived of knowledge* of *their own logic and* by *their own logic*—a logic reduced to a calculation without remainder and leading as well to a market of fools.

Why and how can, however, researchers such as Yann Moulier-Boutang or Maurizio Lazzarato nevertheless perceive in this cerebral or cognitive capitalism[4] an element of novelty opening onto some kind of alternative? My thesis (if not theirs) is that here, that is, with what has also been called *reticulated capitalism*, where the *pharmakon* constitutes a collaborative and dialogical milieu, a genuine mutation of grammatization has occurred: digital reticulation, whereby cognitive activities are themselves proletarianized, constitutes a rupture through which *associated milieus* are formed, that is, milieus of individuation running counter to the processes of dissociation and disindividuation in which proletarianization consists.

It is within this reticulated milieu that what Pekka Himanen calls a "hacker ethics"[5] could appear, and could open the field for a new struggle: *a struggle for abstraction* opposing the class of hackers to those that McKenzie Wark calls the vectorialists.[6] Himanen and Wark show—from a neo-Weberian viewpoint for the former and a post-Marxist and Situationist one for the latter—that the digital *pharmakon*, which makes possible the proletarianization of the nervous system, is *also* what introduces the possibility of a new regime of psychic and collective individuation and, with it, the possibility of a new process of transindividuation opening onto an unprecedented politico-economic perspective: an economy of contribution.

If dissociation results from short-circuits in transindividuation made possible by the *pharmakon* emerging from that process of grammatization in which, in the epoch of reticulated capitalism, cognitive technologies and digitalized cultural technologies are formed, then the formation of an *associated sociotechnical milieu* is the alternative to this poisonous becoming of grammatization. Such an alternative presupposes, however, a veritable revolution of the dominant industrial model—which may fall short of an *overthrow* [*renversement*] of capitalism, but which would certainly be a *revolution* of capitalism.

The question of association and dissociation is also the question of the formation of what in economics are called "externalities." When Yann Moulier-Boutang takes up the metaphor of pollination,[7] what he is describing is tied to the formation of digital reticulation and constitutes a mutation in the process of grammatization, and engenders a *positive pharmacological externality*: an associated sociotechnical milieu in which struggles are waged against the effects of the spread of dissociated milieus, that is, proletarianized milieus, those engendering on the contrary the spread of negative externalities and pharmacological toxicity,[8] that is, a generalized environmental destruction affecting not only the natural and geophysical environment but equally the mental and psychosocial milieus as well.

The associated sociotechnological milieu allows struggles to be waged against these environmental destructions brought about by the "vectorialists" and opens a field of industrial and commercial relations which nullifies the producer/consumer opposition, and which as such breaks precisely with the destruction of commerce by the market: it constitutes a *new commerce*, that is, a new regime of psychic and collective individuation, producing long circuits of transindividuation—the contributors are those who contribute to this creation of long circuits.

This milieu is nevertheless capable of implementing logics of dissociation—and this is why *dialogical*[9] and *as such therapeutic struggles* must be waged with the *pharmakon* of abstraction, which amounts to a matter of taking care of the new commerce.

The associated milieu which is formed in digital reticulation is a specific type of positive externality: technological, industrial, emerging from the most recent stage of grammatization, cognitive and symbolic, that is, restoring to *ratio* its *noetic* dimension, because it constitutes a dialogical relational space in which *psychopower* can be thrown over to become *noopolitics*, or in which the *pharmakon* can be put into the service of an economy of contribution, that is, of a psychosocial therapeutic—given that to economize means before anything else to take care,[10] domestically as well as politically.

50

Otium *and positive externalities: intermittence*

Within the associated sociotechnical milieu, the functional opposition between production and consumption has become obsolete, and externalities must be economically *cultivated* and valorized, even though, like values, they cannot be reduced to the calculability of the economic indicators of a market economy: they require a new conception of economic value, and of its *measurement*, such that it is not reducible to *calculation*. This *culture* is a libidinal as well as a commercial economy, which requires new mutualization mechanisms, a new form of governmental power, and new objects of public property.

In this regard, the two works by Maurizio Lazzarato in which he analyzes the stakes of the struggle waged by the intermittent performing arts workers [*intermittents du spectacle*] to maintain their status (which had in June 2003 been called into question by the French government, who were pressured to do so by employers), have an importance extending beyond the field of the artistic professions. Following the publication of a survey conducted in collaboration with the "Coordination des Intermittents et Précaires," Antonella Corsani and Maurizio Lazzarato state:

. . . the struggle against the reform of the model for unemployment benefits is in reality a struggle whose stakes are those of the use of time. To the injunction to increase the amount of time spent in employment [which is the employers' prescription motivating the calling into question of the status of intermittents], that is, the time of one's life spent employed on the job, the experience of intermittence opposed the plurality of employment times.[11]

The question of time spent working cannot be reduced, in other words, to the question of time in employment, and

. . . to speak seriously about increasing or reducing time spent working means taking into account the totality of these various temporalities.[12]

The French law reducing the working week to thirty-five hours completely ignores this question. One result of this law was an increase in the time devoted to consumption, as Rifkin underlined as early as 2006[13]—but there was no increase in the amount of time spent working in other ways, ways lying outside the scope of employment time. These other efforts, beyond the time of employment, belong within the realm of what the

Romans cultivated as *otium*, a word which Jean-Marie André, in his analysis of its occurrence during the time of the Scipiones, translates as "*studious leisure.*"[14]

Otium, which emerged from Roman culture and originated from a military context, and which then came to represent the noble aspect of the time of human activity—which in *Mécréance et discrédit 1* I have tried to show is the *time of noetic intermittence*[15]—is the condition of possibility of *neg-otium*, that is, employment time. It is because the soul can only be *actually* noetic for *intermittent periods*, and is therefore as such constituted as a "being-only-in-intermittence," behaving most of the time on the contrary like a sensitive or even a vegetative soul, that the "intermittents" (the occasional workers in theatre, film and television) ceaselessly oscillate between on the one hand the calculable employment of their noetic knowledge, this knowledge then being remunerated, that is, *traded* [négocié], and on the other hand the actual development of this knowledge. And it is this noeticity that the destruction of intermittence (of the "intermittents") then eliminates and proletarianizes, that is, instrumentalizes—in order to profit the culture industries.

The time of the passage to the noetic act is that of *otium*, which does not at all mean idle time, yet does mean the time of leisure, that is, of freedom and of "care of the self." *Otium,* from an economic perspective inscribed in a general economy (in the sense in which Georges Bataille deploys this term)—for which it would be an epoch tied to a particular development of *hypomnemata,* that is, an epoch of grammatization, supporting techniques of the self (as shown by Foucault)—and for a political economy inscribed within a libidinal economy encompassing it, constitutes an *externality* opening *the space of human commerce insofar as it is a process of psychic and collective individuation in which long circuits of transindividuation are formed. Neg-otium,* on the other hand, constitutes an economy which is *internalizable via an accounting* (the possibility of which itself stems from *hypomnemata*) of what is calculable for a businessman, and negotiable on a market, all sense of measure (*la mesure,* that is, measure, moderation, or tempo; in Greek, *metron,* that is, also, reserve and rhythm) being reduced to this calculation.

What Corsani and Lazzarato describe as the conjunction of employment time (that is, of the labor internalized by the employer) and work time (as technique of the self) amounts to the economy of *negotium* and *otium,* insofar as these can be grasped as the terms of what Simondon calls a transductive relationship, according to which the terms are constituted through their *individuating tension.*

The way in which we observe intermittent workers spend-
ing their time obliges us to leave behind the binary logic
opposing employment and unemployment, the active and
the inactive, and obliges us to question the very category
of "work." If activity is also exercised during periods of
so-called unemployment or, yet again, during the course of
one's so-called lifetime, during so-called free time, during
the time spent on training and education, right up to the
point at which it becomes the time of rest, then what is
covered over by the concept of "work," since within it
can be found a plurality of activities and heterogeneous
temporalities?[16]

These analyses show that it is not sufficient to pose the
question of work in the terms that were fashionable
in the 1990s, when the reality of chronic unemployment forced a reflection on the structural consequences
of productivity increases. Beyond these terms, it is a
matter of a change in the industrial model, a change
which would also constitute the dawn of an age of a new
conception of work, which must not be confused with
employment, and which, as the consumerist model falls
apart, requires the invention of a new social temporality,
and, as Lazzarato has shown, redefines the question of
what Robert Castel calls social property.[17]

What this raises, then, but in entirely new terms,

is the question of a negative tax such as was proposed by Jeremy Rifkin—and then taken up by Michel Rocard[18]—in order to support the development of a "social sector," a sector defined as being non-economic insofar as it is non-market. Now, *this is not at all a question of bringing the economy to an end*, but of thinking an *other* economy, and of overcoming a consumerism within which the purchasing power produced by employment in fact destroys work and all forms of knowledge in the epoch of the generalized proletarianization of producers as well as consumers.

The flaw in Rifkin's proposal lies in the fact that his consideration of the economic circuit does not include the question of *otium* or of knowledge in all its forms. On the other hand, the notion of a negative tax as a mutualized support for the development of positive externalities, and through the development of a new form of social property, finds in the granting of unemployment benefits to intermittent workers in the performing arts a model which is particularly well adapted to the change which is currently underway: this is made clear by reading the works of Corsani and Lazzarato. But it cannot be a matter of limiting such proposals merely to the spheres of art, culture and "creative workers": it is the social and economic industrial model as a totality that must be rethought.

Desolidarization and negative externalities

The reconstruction of positive externalities and the support of work practices stemming from *otium* (that is, from noetic intermittence) is the necessary condition for the reconstitution of long circuits of transindividuation, which are themselves the only possibility of struggling against the spread of negative externalities. The extent of the spread of negative externalities is now being discovered by the world, as consumerism falls apart and as environmental disequilibrium becomes a planetary obsession. Among the forms of this disequlibrium must be counted the destructive effects that the dictatorship of short-termism—exerted upon every society by marketing—brings to bear on the public sphere (on political space and time) as well as on the private sphere, leading to the pure and simple *liquidation of social relations.*

It is in this context that one can see—in Belgium for example, where the Flemish exclude from public housing anyone who cannot speak Dutch—how short-circuits in transindividuation have destroyed the individuation of reference[19] permitting two linguistic psychosocial individuation processes to refer to the same process of political and territorial individuation, so as to coalesce within one nation. These ruinous effects of dissociation and of such short-circuits, which are the inverse of what occurs in associated milieus, can be seen in the politico-linguistic opposition between the Flemish and the Walloons.

Instead of the individuation of reference, the global culture industries have substituted the behavioral prescriptions of marketing, which *liquidate solidarities*:

- firstly, in the territorial space of contemporaneity: the Flemish withdraw their solidarity from the Belgian Walloons, leading to the destruction of their political space;
- secondly, in the generational time of contemporaneity: harnessing [*captation*] the attention of a generation cuts it off from other generations, engendering short-circuits in the transindividuation of generations – primary identification, for example, fails to take place within the juvenile psychic apparatus, or adult consumers, unable to afford the costs of educating their children, somehow manage, nevertheless, to buy expensive cars.

It is this very process of desolidarization that lies behind the decline of market value occurring today, market capitalization having been ruined by the collapse to which a capitalism which has become drive-based [*pulsionnel*] and speculative inevitably leads. One of the most violent effects of this process is the pauperization of youth, unleashing the threat of an economic confrontation between the generations at the very moment when the intergenerational symbolic bond capable of containing such a threat has been short-circuited in the process of transindividuation.

All this results in generalized irresponsibility, such that the spread of dissociated milieus becomes necessarily correlated with the spread of negative externalities. Dissociated milieus, as factors disconnecting the psychic individual from their relation to collective individuation and, correlatively, as factors destroying investment in all its forms (for which financial speculation and drive-based obsessions are substituted) engender toxic behavior in every sphere of society, dominated by a structural short-termism to the precise extent that drives and speculation are intrinsically short-term.

The short-term tendency, induced by the liquidation of responsibility, desublimation and extreme disenchantment, is the most immediate consequence of the tendential fall of the rate of profit, combined as it is with the tendential fall of libidinal energy and the spread of what René Passet calls passages to the limit, that is, processes through which the functioning of systems leads to the destruction of the very conditions of this functioning, processes which are ineluctably translated into a runaway increase in negative externalities.

The bourgeoisie swept away by the mafia

The historical failure of communism was due to the fact that it could not think association, that is, it renounced the struggle against proletarianization as loss of knowledge, and against the short-circuits in transindividuation that are clearly characteristics of Stalinist bureaucratic totalitarianism, just as they are of the totalization that is conduced by marketing: it is only in terms of ways of dissociating that capitalism and communism have distinguished themselves from one another. Even those Marxists who were situated outside of Stalinism, and who were against Stalin, were never able to manage a critique of dissociation, because from the beginning they confused proletarianization and pauperization.

In the communist world, this dissociation led, intrinsically and structurally, to the totalitarian negation of structures of existence, which for a long time was not the case for capitalism, especially when it combined Fordism with Keynesianism.[20] Capitalism, unlike communism, for a long time favored the constitution of motivational systems based on these structures of existence, structures that it nevertheless harnessed, exploited and finally destroyed, but by means which were indeed effective, and that even constituted a new libidinal economy and new perspectives of sublimation, contrary to communist dissociation.[21] Yet it remains the case that capitalism would in the end become a process of dissociation leading ineluctably to demotivation:[22] it was condemned to encounter its limit in the tendential fall in libidinal energy which it had itself provoked.

At this point it is necessary to return to the question of commerce. Political economy is a way of organizing transindividuation not only at the level of symbolic exchange, but also at the level of the exchange of commodities. Once, while in Beijing, the taxi in which I was riding drove past a store selling plastic mannequins, and what surprised me was that such a business could have been created by a Chinese shop owner in this purportedly communist economy, an economy which functions as powerfully as it does only insofar as within it psychic individuation is controlled by a collective individuation *without intermediaries*, that is, de-psychologized, short-circuiting transindividuation, and therefore disindividuated, disindividuating, and destructive of all motives.

The capitalist economy strictly speaking *no longer works*, because it wants the psychic individual to be self-directed, to become the "entrepreneur of itself,"[23] without collective individuation, but rather through a collective disindividuation orchestrated by marketing, which exploits the possibilities of control emanating from the provoking of short-circuits, and, since the "conservative revolution" and neoliberalism (and the project of "refounding" Medef which amounts to the French translation of neoliberalism), through a government of inequalities which ruins the social—all of which destroys the economic milieu itself, which thereby becomes a "dis-economy," leading finally to the liquidation of intermediation, which is the translation of transindividuation into the economic sphere and in its commercial form (all the more true given that "competition" leads in reality to the growth of monopolies).

Desublimation—which thus leads and in the same movement to the spread of negative externalities, to the liquidation of commerce by the market and to the destruction of social connectedness—can be translated by the fact that the bourgeoisie is swept away by the mafia, which is the fate befalling the former communist countries, but also of all drive-based capitalism.

The mafia tends to replace the bourgeoisie and capitalism takes on an essentially mafia-like character from the moment that the disenchantment of the world is completed. This disenchantment becomes, then, no longer *relative* but *absolute*: there can *no longer be any relative re-enchantment*—as was, for example, the advent of modern art (rejecting the "industrial art" of which Flaubert speaks through the character of Jacques Arnoux),[24] both *within and for bourgeois modernity*. When disenchantment becomes absolute, the power of the powerful plays out *without consistence*, without relation to *otium* of any kind, without the slightest belief, and therefore as absolute *cynicism*: with neither faith nor law.

It is within this epoch of mafia capitalism—that is, of a capitalism without bourgeoisie—that one sees develop the systematic state lie, drive-based politics, and an addictive consumerism induced by industrial populism. If fascism is a disease of bourgeois capitalism, the occurrence of which is a warning sign foreshadowing absolute disenchantment, then the becoming mafia of capitalism is not an accident which would be more or less epiphenomenal: rather, it is the normal and everyday functioning of such a capitalism. In this respect, Sarkozyism is not, unfortunately, if one can put it like this, a return of Petainism: it is something far more serious, more complex and more difficult to think than the return of the same old song.

The middle classes will soon disappear, because

they have been proletarianized by the development of consumerism. This is not to say that they have been pauperized: the former is not the consequence of the latter. It is to say that the middle classes are no longer any kind of "petty bourgeoisie"—not because they have been pauperized, but through a *symbolic misery* [*misère symbolique*: symbolic impoverishment or immiseration] and through an *aesthetic and noetic proletarianization*: without *otium*, without access for example to that instrumental practice which was such a delight to Roland Barthes, for whom a true appreciation of the music of Schumann can only derive from its interpretation, that is, from the practice of playing it on the piano, as he explains in "Musica practica,"[25] a sentiment which also lies behind the refrain constantly repeated to Pierre Schaeffer by his father:

Work on your instrument!

In so doing, Schaeffer's father reminds us that *otium* is work, that work always involves an instrument, and hence that so too does *otium*.

The petty bourgeoisie, even though it is not rich, nevertheless belongs to the bourgeoisie insofar as it has access to something beyond subsistence, and can emancipate itself from the pure necessity of reproducing its labor power, and can therefore liberate itself from pure *negotium*, that is, from completely calculable exchange: the petty bourgeois are able to be music lovers [*amateurs de musique*]. What was once the privilege of the nobility became, in the nineteenth century, *par excellence* that of the bourgeoisie, then became as well the privilege of the petty bourgeoisie.

This is what was liquidated by the extension of consumerism to all social classes. Through what I have described, with Nicolas Donin, as a mechanical turn in sensibility,[26] condition of possibility of this age of the *pharmakon* constituted by the psycho-technologies of psycho-power,[27] consumerism transforms everything into needs, that is, into subsistence, and liquidates desire, that is, objects of *otium* and sublimation, including for the highest levels of the bourgeoisie who *thus* become a mafia. And as for the *wage-earners of the ideal* [*les salariés de l'idéal*], as Jean-Claude Milner calls university professors,[28] they too are unable to escape this fate.

Now, the libidinal and political economies of contribution that are reconstituted in associated milieus tend toward the reopening of this dimension, which is that of consistencies and of what I have called an *otium of the people*.[29] Only *otium* can reconstitute credit, that is, an economy: there is no economy other than when it is projected into an investment. This reopens for the contemporary retentional system the question of *protention*—because an economy, whether libidinal or political, is always an economy of protention.

Economy of protentions, permanent revolution, and contribution

Economic systems in general, and the capitalist system in particular, always constitute systems of production of protentions. This protention production system clearly achieves greater efficiency with the appearance of a very particular case of grammatization: money, the word for which in Latin evokes *Mnémosunè*.[30] In spite of that, the question of protention cannot be reduced to the question of fiduciary credit: it is rooted in a retentional ensemble, and this ensemble is constituted as much by machines and by the souls of producers and consumers as it is by money—money which, like all forms of retention, converts time into space, but which clearly does so in a very specific sense.

If capitalism is a protention production system which in terms of its performativity is very remarkable—thus when one says that the stockmarket has lost so many billions of dollars in the course of such and such a crisis, this means that a power of active protentions, a power of the *action* of protentions (of anticipations), has been lost by the *credit system*[31]—then the economy of contribution is a new economic arrangement (libidinal and political) between grammatized retentions and protentions of investment.

The capitalist system for creating protentions is a system of credit which brings about a change in the system of belief—by turning belief into something calculable, and by therefore engendering something better than belief (at least in the eyes of *negotium*): trust [*confiance*]. Credit in general, in all its forms—whether banking, religious, scientific, literary, artistic, political, or social—is the organization of protentions. Credit is the concrete social expression of protentions *which realize themselves*, which *perform*, as one could say, adapting Austin's theory of performativity to the question of credit performance such as it has led to the transformation of matter, social relations and behavior—that is, of *wills*, and from which proceeds the extraordinary permanent revolution in which capitalism since the industrial revolution has consisted.[32]

What took place during the course of the nineteenth and twentieth centuries was the organization of the capitalist "protention-alization" of the world, which consisted firstly in the disenchantment of the legitimating powers and the secularization of beliefs: not in their destruction, but in their transformation into calculable beliefs, including through the harnessing of scientific beliefs by the production apparatus in order to devise ways of transforming matter, nature, technique, human beings, and behavior. This transformation of belief was able to accomplish enormous gains in productivity throughout the nineteenth century, enabling new forms of membership and social cohesion within the social project, carried out by the bourgeoisie through the development of schools, through the engagement it made possible with national history, etc.

In the twentieth century, the mobilization of libidinal energies took place through the capturing and harnessing of protentions via the channeling of attention. It was thus a matter of *elaborating* [*tendre*] an *industrial protention*: of causing the tensions accumulated in the protentions of consumers to reach out [*tendre*] toward industrial products, products which are the "realization" of the protentions of producers, with the goal of causing the protentions of consumers and producers to converge, and thus of overcoming the contradiction in which consists the tendential fall in the rate of profit.

In the course of the recent crisis, this protentional system collapsed, after having run out of control as it was driven toward an ever-more extreme short-termism, eventually reaching the limit of its *self-annihilation* (a short-term tendency, when accomplished to the point of perfection, leads to the destruction of the retentional time in which knowledge consists, as well as the destruction of the protentional time in which investment consists). This collapse of protentions was inscribed in the fate of consumerist capitalism to the precise extent that this form of capitalism depended on the proletarianization of retention in which the control of attention consists, a proletarianization amounting to a loss of knowledge, and a loss affecting consumption as much as production.

The intermittent workers of the performing arts, and all those whom Jean-Claude Milner calls the wage-earners of the ideal, continue to cultivate a relationship to the *pharmakon*, in order that they may *still* pass into the noetic act, from which they draw a distinct pleasure that cannot be considered to be mere enjoyment, given that it consists in a feeling of *infinite différance*.

The new work practices being developed on the networks of the associated sociotechnical milieu, however, themselves also tend toward the passage to the noetic act, a goal which, essentially, is their motive. Such a motive amounts to a protention. And such a state of fact awaits only one thing: for its constitution as a state of law in order that retentional systems may be placed into the service of this protentional activity. And it is to this question of a law such as this that a new critique of political economy must be consecrated—and this is so to the extent that these practices, which are becoming very widespread, reconstitute the economic field in its totality, well beyond the "cultural sector" or the "social sector."

Such are the questions which arise for a critique of political economy restarted on the basis of an analysis of the place of tertiary retention in the economy: these are questions of *pharmacology*, for which an economy of contribution constitutes the *sociotherapy* proper to the contemporary stage of grammatization—it constitutes, in other words, its system of care.

Pharmacology of Capital and Economy of Contribution

For Jean-Michel Salanskis
To the memory of Jean-François Lyotard

The supreme effort of the writer as of the artist only succeeds in partially raising for us the veil of ugliness and insignificance that leaves us uncaring [*incurieux*] before the world. Then, he says to us:

> Look, look
> Fragrant with clover and artemesia
> Holding tight their quick, narrow streams
> The lands of the Aisne and the Oise.

Marcel Proust

On January 25, 2007, while participating in a colloquium devoted to the work of Jean-François Lyotard, I proposed a reading of *The Postmodern Condition* which characterized those traits of capitalism described by Lyotard as typifying a new form of libidinal economy: that form invented by consumerist capitalism in North America at the beginning of the twentieth century.

According to this reading, postmodernity resulted from a consumerist organization of the libido leading eventually to the liquidation of the libido itself, to its "diseconomy," that is, to the liquidation of that libidinal economy which modernity hitherto constituted—a process of liquidation the consequences of which began to appear at the end of the 1970s (*La condition postmoderne* being published at the moment Margaret Thatcher gained power in Great Britain, constituting the beginning of the "conservative revolution").

In the course of my reading, I tried to show why the concepts enabling the thinking of this *consumerist libidinal diseconomy* that is postmodernity were less those of Lyotard's eponymous work[1] than of Freud, whom, therefore, it was a matter of rereading and reinterpreting. I intended to show that Lyotard had in *The Postmodern Condition* opened the possibility of a new thinking of capitalism—and of the extension of proletarianization which everywhere accompanies it—and that this thinking remains to be elaborated, but also that doing so presupposes a critique of the Lyotardian account of "libidinal economy."

In the course of the discussion that followed this intervention, Jean-Michel Salanskis, who with Corine Énaudeau organized the colloquium, told me that he no longer understood what it means to speak of *capitalism*, nor did he understand discourse which continues to convoke this word: he then declared that he could not understand my own discourse.

The present work, like *For a New Critique of Political Economy*, tries to respond to this remark, made to me by my friend shortly before the crisis of capitalism revealed the extent of its disaster in the month of October 2008. The theses advanced here, first presented before the administrative council of Ars Industrialis,[2] then in a public session of this association gathered on December 5, 2009,[3] continue the analysis begun in *For a New Critique of Political Economy*.

74

This work examines two questions:

- How should one understand "profit" in the phrase, "tendential fall in the rate of profit"?
- More generally, what is in play in the concept expressed with this phrase?

There is no tendency without a counter-tendency

What the third volume of *Capital* tries to think with the phrase "tendential fall in the rate of profit"—the stakes of which clearly cannot be measured by referring to the formula $\mathbf{p} = \mathbf{s}/(\mathbf{c}+\mathbf{v})$—is a *negative dynamic* that, Marx posits, would in principle be inherent to a capitalist system formed and held within contradictory tendencies: capitalism would thus be a dynamic system threatened by a limit that would be reached if the bearish tendency to which the very functioning of the profit rate gives rise were to achieve completion [*s'accomplissait*].

This is certainly not how Marxism has interpreted this theory: on the contrary, what Marxism has pronounced in this regard is the *ineluctable* accomplishment of this tendency. And Marx himself probably read it this way. But if there is a tendency for the rate of profit to fall, then there must also be a counter-tendency, as we learn from both Nietzsche and Freud. Were this not the case, we would no longer be speaking of a tendency, but rather of a simple and linear, that is, deterministic, evolution.

That Marxism and Marx himself (and before him the Hegelian dialectic) did not manage to reason this way—in terms of tendencies—is a problem bequeathed by Marx, but that does not invalidate his theory of the bearish tendency of the profit rate.

This way of thinking in terms of tendencies passes through *psychology*, that is, through a discourse on souls, on their logic and their economy: on their logic insofar as it *is* an economy.

Given the necessity of a debate on the tendential fall in the rate of profit, the question is not whether such a tendency exists: rather, it concerns the nature of its counter-tendency (or counter-tendencies). What is really at stake is knowing how to think the play of tendencies.

The profit to which Marx refers is the return on investment

Turning to how the word "profit" should be understood, the question is: if "profit" can be defined as the return on investment, that is, as a function of a system enabling remuneration for invested capital, and hence for risks that are taken, then should this definition of profit include or exclude speculation—which tends to destroy the system of investment, given that, *here, the stake is time,* and, more precisely, that which affects the playing out of the short term and the long term, both *with* one another and *against* one another?

The profit deriving from the financialized economy clearly does not correspond with what Marx calls the rate of profit (**p**), where **p** = **s/(c+v)**. **P** depends on the system of production as constant capital and variable capital. The profits deriving from financialization tend, on the contrary, to decouple from **p** in relation to **s/(c+v)**, and to become essentially speculative profits. They therefore raise the question of what Marx calls "fictitious capital."

Profit, durability, and toxicity

An objection raised against the theory of the tendential fall in the rate of profit is that we have seen capital accumulate enormous gains over the last few decades. But the crisis of 2008 (like those that preceded it, but more than any of the earlier crises) makes it necessary to examine both the nature and the solidity of this profitability—a profitability which during this crisis has come to appear *structurally toxic*.

The question of profit is first of all, and jointly:

- that of its exogenous sustainability, that is, for the rest of society (profits cannot be durable if they destroy society);
- that of its endogenous durability, that is, for capital itself (it must conserve its value over time);
- that of the temporality which it configures, that is, as concerns fictitious capital, the question of the quality of the anticipations in which it consists, given that fictitious capital, insofar as it is a *system of relatively calculated protentions*,[4] is a necessary function of the system, irreducible in this regard to mere speculation, while entrepreneurial investment constitutes yet another type of anticipation.

It is only within such systems of anticipation, which must be qualified and consolidated by rules, that profit can be produced.

Could the gains achieved by Bernard Madoff, estimated at 50 billion dollars, and those of the speculators taken in by him, ever have been realized as profits? Yes, without doubt. But these profits were fraudulent, not very durable, and *purely* toxic, because they were created through doctored anticipations. And for Madoff's clients, they have become dead losses.

When Albert Spaggiari, a criminal who was also a militant of the extreme right, robbed the Société Générale bank in Nice in 1976, thereby accomplishing what has been called "the heist of the century," he made a "profit" of 50 million francs. But these profits have never been recognized as such: rather, they are qualified as theft.

Those who are careless in the pharmacology of capital

Should we conclude that all fictitious capital always tends to produce systems that are toxic, if not fraudulent (that is, *purely* toxic)? The answer is clearly positive: *more than any other human psychotechnique*, fictitious capital is a *pharmakon*[5] and, more precisely, an *accounting game* [*jeu d'écritures*, dummy entries], and the anticipation systems made possible by this *phantasia* of capital presuppose the existence of a free capital which structurally tends to disinvest when it sees its profits decline.[6]

These disinvestments are short-circuits, in just the same way as artificial and hypomnesic memory—that is, the *pharmakon* of writing—can short-circuit living and anamnesic memory.[7]

Let us propose that this tendency leads to *carelessness* [*incurie*]: one calls a speculator (and, in times of war, a "profiteer") someone who scoffs at the economic as well as social consequences of "profitable" decisions. Such a person belongs to the category of those whom one otherwise calls the indifferent, the uncaring, or the *careless* [*incurieux*]:[8] those "who are not bothered" ["*qui ni'en ont cure*"], that is, who "don't have anything to do" with anything—those who say, "*I don't care.*" Those who mock the world.

It is because there is such a *tendency to carelessness,* and because it is *irreducible,* being inscribed within this pharmacology, that regulatory systems are imposed, which aim to *limit* the destructive effects of this speculative tendency of free capital—and to keep a *sufficient and steady hold on things, that is, on investment,* given the instability of capital circulation.

In the capitalist economic system, the circulation of free capital is supposed to measure the *credit* that the financial sub-system accords to such and such an economic actor within the production sub-system—and, through this system of measurement, establish the belief that "society" invests in this activity. The circulation of free capital is a specific protentional organization resting on a complex, fallible and corruptible system of *pharmaka,* in which one finds money, actions and obligations, various financial instruments, ratings agencies, etc.

This capital, however, tends to become purely speculative when it no longer measures a capital of confidence in the future of the assets of the production apparatus—in relation to which it constitutes, as a system of anticipations, capacities for investment—but instead relies on operations which are either purely self-referential (such that the anticipations created by the financial sub-system anticipate nothing but itself and come at the expense of the production system), or else are oriented toward the production apparatus, but are structurally short-term (that is, based on disinvestment, that is, on the *pillage* of the production apparatus).

Innovation, short-termism, and speculation

Let us now return to productive capital.

A common objection to the thesis of the tendential fall in the profit rate is that the technical innovation lying at the heart of the production apparatus enables the system to ceaselessly stimulate its differentiation, with constant capital thereby conferring a competitive advantage upon the innovative entrepreneur.

The question of innovation, however, is not only

a matter of conception and production as entrepreneurs transfer technological inventions and scientific discoveries onto their businesses: innovation is also and before anything else the *socialization* of innovation—that is, the transformation of society. Now, in the twentieth century this transformation operated through the organization of consumption, that is, through the implementation of apparatuses for society's *adaptation* to techno-industrial change, but not as the *adoption* of innovation by society.

It would be a matter of adoption if techno-industrial change was co-produced by society itself. But the organization of consumption presupposes, on the contrary, that the becoming of *social systems* must *structurally submit* to the becoming of the *economic system,* something enabled by granting the latter full control over technological becoming, that is, over the *technical system*—this submission being obtained by capturing and harnessing the attention of consumers, by diverting their libidinal energy toward objects of innovation, and by controlling their behavior via marketing.

Now, such harnessing of libidinal energy leads to its destruction: it submits to calculation that which, as object of desire, is only constituted through becoming infinitized, that is, through surpassing all calculation.

This destruction of desire leads to a drive-based

"frustration," forming a system with what, in twentieth-century consumerist society, conditions the social absorption of innovation described by Schumpeter as "economic evolution," leading to the installation of a system tending to produce *chronic and structural obsolescence*, a system for which the *normal* relation to objects becomes *disposability*.[9] And if financialization constitutes an aspect of that system, then both businesses (as constant capital) and workers (as variable capital) become as structurally disposable as any other object of consumption.

Consumption becomes, therefore, both an expedient and an outlet—a *pharmakon*—aggravating frustration by displacing it on a very short-term basis toward the newest object of consumption produced by this "permanent innovation." Novelty is thus systematically valorized at the expense of durability, and this *organization of detachment, that is, of unfaithfulness or infidelity*[10] (equally called flexibility),[11] contributes to the decomposition of the libidinal economy, to the spread of drive-based behaviors and to the liquidation of social systems.

At the foundation of this systemic organization of *infidelity*—which is concretely expressed as much by the liquidation of primary identification[12] and the modification of infantile synaptogenesis[13] as by those short-circuits induced in society that I have described as "dissociation"[14]—the systems of anticipation of free capital and the hyperlabile behavior of consumers act in harmony and are "potentized" [*potentialisent*], in the sense that combining drugs can *potentize* [*potentialiser*] their curative but also their toxic effects (as when, for instance, alcohol is combined with psychotropes or anti-inflammatories).

Anticipations of free capital and consumer behavior therefore become correlatively and *systemically short-termist, speculative and drive-based.*

Economy of protentions

Fictitious capital is a system of anticipations and gambles *which can only make judgments about illusions,* that is, speculations and calculations about future possibilities *which may never be realized.* It is this system of projection of protentions which, as the organization of risk-taking (more or less limited), gives the capitalist system its dynamic: capitalism presupposes the existence of free capital open to speculation understood in this sense.

The "advance" on reality that produces these anticipations, however, such that they are structurally exposed to speculation, must proceed before anything else from a *motivation*, itself inscribed within an *economy of motivations*, which is also an economy of fantasy: such an economy is what produces protean libidinal energy or, to express it in more precisely psychoanalytical terms, polymorphous libidinal energy.

This polymorphism must be unified by what Max Weber called a spirit: it presupposes an investment in a libidinal economy which in some way confers upon it its symbolic calibration, and its constitution within a system of exchange forming a polymorphous social commerce.

Such are the questions pervading *The New Spirit of Capitalism*, in which Luc Boltanski and Eve Chiapello refer to both Max Weber and Albert Hirschman in order to show that:

> systemic constraints [which are exercised on all the actors within the capitalist system] are insufficient on their own to elicit their engagement. Duress [*contrainte*] must be internalized and justified.[15]

In other words, it presupposes that a libidinal economy keeps in reserve *an exchangeable libidinal energy*, which bestows consistency on the "advance" that the system makes upon itself, and as its dynamic, throughout the various forms of motivation that it elicits.

In the libidinal economy, the "advance"—the protentional structure of this economy[16]—is constituted by desire, and such desire is structurally infinite, that is, incalculable, to the extent that it tends to "infinitize" its objects: the libidinal economy is the economy of this infinitization and as such constitutes a system of intrinsically long-term care.

Conversely, the destruction of this advance founded on desire, that is, on symbolic capital—a destruction induced by the "finitization" of its objects, and as the organization of their intrinsic disposability, including workers and businesses—destroys motivation itself in *all* its forms.

It thus becomes an advance based on the drives. But given that the drives are by nature short-termist, this leads to disinvestment, that is, to the destruction of profitability understood as *benefit*: it leads to the destruction of profitability understood as the consolidation of the dynamism and durability of the system, as that which *does* the system *good* [*ce qui* fait du bien *au système*].

*Consumerist capital and funny money [*monnaie de singe*]: the mathematization of carelessness*

The tendential fall in the rate of profit which haunted the productivist system characteristic of the nineteenth century and of European industrialization (and which provoked several crises) was absorbed at the beginning of the twentieth century, in North America, by a counter-tendency obtained through the consumerist organization of the libidinal economy: by the establishment of a system of protentions directed by capital from the side of consumption in functional and direct relation to free capital invested and "protentionalized" in this sense. The implementation of the consumerist society was the principal response that the American economy found to this systemic tendency—and this form of capitalism therefore cannot be thought with Marxist concepts alone.

It was within this emerging context, as the productivist industrial model became consumerist, that in 1913 Schumpeter wrote his evolutionary theory of the capitalist economy. Ford then constitutes the perfect example of this ideal-type that Schumpeter calls the entrepreneur (Weber having himself supplied a first version of this ideal-type through the figure of the entrepreneur of Pennsylvania).[17] But Fordist entrepreneurial innovation, based on Taylorism, presupposes the organization of mass consumption—the harnessing and exploitation of libidinal energy in the service of constant behavioral control. It is for this reason that this form of capitalism requires the mobilization of Freudian concepts.

This consumerist counter-tendency—invented as a way of struggling against the tendential fall in the rate of profit, and implemented via a function of the system of which Marx was unaware, that is, marketing, and which led to the reorganization of fictitious capital and to the fact that the manner of controlling production shifts from entrepreneurial control to *shareholder* management—this counter-tendency in turn becomes bearish toward the end of the twentieth century, and does so at the very moment that buying power diminishes, everywhere setting up a massive process of pauperization, reconstituting the characteristic traits of the nineteenth century.

Having destroyed the libidinal economy upon which it was founded, the consumerist counter-tendency then systemically aggravates the toxicity of financial pharmacology, that is, the tendency, itself drive-based and short-termist, of fictitious capital, accentuating pauperization in all layers of the population as well as undermining the apparatus of production, which is pillaged via leveraged buyouts and other speculative techniques directed specifically against businesses.

The struggle against the tendential fall in the rate of profit thus induces a tendential fall in libidinal energy, which reinforces the speculative tendency of capital, that is, its disinvestment, thereby undermining profit. The enormous accumulation of capital tends therefore to be transformed into funny money [*monnaie de singe*]—and the pension fund system appears for what it is: one pole of a system, called fictitious capital, such that, *having mathematized its pharmacological tendency to carelessness*, its other pole is constituted by deceptions [*leurres*] *deliberately* organizing the dilution of responsibility, deceptions with names such as "subprime," "securitization," "Bernard Madoff," etc.

The short-termist macro-tendency

If the way in which Marx calculated the rate of profit failed to take the speculative tendency in which fictitious capital essentially consists fully into account, this only serves to show, precisely that the capitalist investment system is subject, as a dynamic system, *either* to a bearish tendency, *or* to a speculative functioning which necessarily becomes destructive and false.

Schumpeter contradicts this perspective by showing how innovation *functionally articulates* productive capital and fictitious capital—as risk capital oriented toward "technological values." But Schumpeter does not integrate the question of consumption as the harnessing of libidinal energy, nor the bearish effects that this harnessing induces over this energy form essential to consumerist capitalism, nor the reinforcement of the tendency toward short-termist carelessness that these effects inevitably provoke in fictitious capital.

In order to describe, then, the functioning of the apparatus of production—such as it is motored by a permanent innovation requiring an organization of consumption by the apparatus of psychopower that marketing constitutes, even if one retains from Marx the separation of fictitious from productive capital in his formulation of the calculation of $\mathbf{p}$—we would need to:

1. add to his formula an innovation function and a consumption function, in order to describe an apparatus of production which, today, is no longer merely productivist, but consumerist;
2. integrate a tendential fall in libidinal energy, that is, a tendency for the libido to decompose into its component drives.

If, in addition, one admits:

- that fictitious capital is essential to the system as it is the organization of calculable anticipations;
- that it is constituted by a structurally short-termist tendency, that is, by a tendency to carelessness which, in the consumerist industrial model, forms a system with an increasing obsolescence of products and services, produced by a constant acceleration of the processes of innovation and technological transfer, and by a correlative aggressiveness of marketing;

then it appears evident that the consumerist model has reached its limits because it accommodates a *short-termist macro-tendency*, which in future can only lead to closing the system off from any future, that is, to a blockage of the processes of anticipation, whether entrepreneurial or financial, and to a generalized degradation of social and psychic motivations, but equally of *economic* motivations.

Given the existence of such a macro-tendency, the question becomes to know what the *macro-counter-tendency* might be.

Shareholder capitalism as systemic carelessness

To questions of durability and sustainability, and of safeguarding the dynamic system that capitalism is as a system of motivations, must be added the problem of negative externalities: the crisis of 2008 coincides with the fulfillment of the predictions of the Meadows report and of René Passet, namely, that the consumerist industrial model is condemned to overshoot its own limits by destroying geological resources and geographical and meteorological systems, all while provoking a demographic explosion.

This destruction of physical systems is combined with the destruction of psychic and social systems, which are the conditions of production of all libidinal energy—that of producers as well as designers, investors and consumers. The profit *rate* then tends very certainly to fall, while the "profit" is only maintained at high levels because it has become intrinsically speculative and careless—either through ruinous instruments of financial pharmacology, or by frankly Mafia-esque operations, indeed ones that are manifestly criminal and strictly illegal.

In this case, what is augmented is a profit that no longer bears any relation to the profit rate calculated by **p**, since capital, in the face of the eventual obsolescence of innovation itself, and taking into account the essentially drive-based character of consumption, tends to become structurally fictitious, that is, to be tied neither to **c** nor to **v** in the definition which supports the calculation **s/(c+v)**: it is this tendency which is concretely expressed in management becoming shareholder-based—of which the Forgeart/EADS insider trading scandal revealed calamitous effects—and which installs a genuinely systemic carelessness.

Economy of excessiveness [démesure] and infinite responsibility

However speculative this fictitious capital might be, it measures anticipations, making them relatively calculable. Protentions of psychosocial temporality, however, are not absolutely calculable, and always exceed relative anticipations: they emerge from a libidinal economy that infinitizes itself, that is, an *economy of excessiveness* that produces a psychosocial *will*, otherwise called motivation, that is, that produces *motives for existing*, otherwise called meaning, and which presupposes what Simondon names the transindividual—founded on a process of transindividuation in which protentions are elaborated into the formation of long circuits.[18]

In other words, the protention that constitutes psychosocial temporality presupposes that the assumption of an *infinite responsibility* will come to "back up" this temporality as a kind of *credit*, where credit cannot be reduced to trust [*confiance*] understood as calculation,[19] but presupposes a desire invested in an infinitizable object.

At the origin of capitalism, it was the God of reformed monotheism who assumed the symbolic function of this infinite responsibility, as we are informed by Weber. But what could take on the symbolic function of this infinite responsibility when capitalism turns into a process of disenchantment, nihilism and the death of God? In what then will this relation to infinity consist, a relation which speculation tends to dilute, and to liquidate (through which, however, it is the system itself which becomes diluted—the mutualization of losses only allowing social and psychic systems to absorb this dilution by destroying them a little more, that is, by diluting themselves in order to preserve the financial sub-system within the capitalist economic system, and always to the detriment of the production sub-system)?[20]

This infinite object is that of desire. What both Freud and Nietzsche gave us to think—and what they gave us to think as the play of tendencies—in the functioning of what the Viennese analyst will call the psychic apparatus, is that the *psyche* is intrinsically constituted by its relation to infinity. This infinity is that object of infinite desire which, even though it does not exist (it is a fantasy), nevertheless *consists*.

Such consistence alone allows a general economy to perpetuate, that is, to exceed speculative finitude—a finitude which is encountered when speculation, calculating and measuring anticipations, proves intrinsically careless because it has become the incarnation of a short-termist, that is, drive-based, tendency. These are also the stakes of general economy according to Georges Bataille.

From the moment that American capitalism implements the "American way of life" as a new libidinal economy through the psychopower of marketing, it can only make this infinity, which is infinite *desire*, function by finitizing it, that is, by destroying the apparatus of production of libidinal energy and of all sublimatory by-products. It can therefore only cause its dysfunction.

The implementation of this psychopower, however, which believes at the same time in the doctrine of *soft power*, will for a long time contain its finitizing effects through a public power theorized by Keynes and materialized by Roosevelt. This public power, called the *welfare state,* will:

- on the one hand, maintain, beneath psychopower, social and sublimatory systems for the production of libidinal energy, in particular as educational systems;
- on the other hand, limit the speculative tendencies of fictitious capital that this psychopower reinforces, through the roles of regulation and adjustment assumed by the public power when faced with the effects of disadjustments engendered by the incessant mutations of the industrial technical system, which destabilizes other social systems.

To say this another way, the welfare state is not merely an avatar of biopower: added to it is the question of psychopower. This is the character of the state in the epoch of what Adorno and Horkheimer will call the culture industry—and in the epoch when these industries, vectors of the American way of life, begin to fight over the *leadership* of social change.

The "conservative revolution" as subordination of the technical system to the economic system

Three crucial points must here be emphasized:

1. Before marketing and fictitious capital took control of industrial becoming and before the mass media

96

became thoroughly drive-based, that is, at the beginning of the 1970s, the profit rate of businesses bottomed out—an economic fact which meant that at that time it was difficult to argue that the tendential fall in the rate of profit was an absurd proposition.

2. It was in order to reverse this situation, installed throughout the Western world by Keynesianism, that the "conservative revolution" was implemented by Margaret Thatcher in England from 1979 and by Ronald Reagan in North America from 1980—the system based on the Bretton Woods agreement having been abandoned in 1971, the American apparatus of production having drastically regressed just as had occurred to the former British empire, and the "conservative revolution" aiming to "financialize" and to globalize Western capitalism, in order to ensure that it continued to direct the course of globalization (a strategy which was a lamentable failure).

3. This calling into question of the state—which took the form of denouncing the welfare state on the grounds it destroys individual responsibility, and hence that government had become "the problem and not the solution" (to paraphrase Reagan)—had the goal of making it possible for capital to completely

direct (via the intermediary of psychopower implemented through marketing) the course of what Bertrand Gille called the disadjustment between the technical system and the other human systems, a role which from the beginning of the industrial revolution right up until that moment had belonged to government.

In other words, after the "conservative revolution," the becoming of the technical system in the course of globalization (leading to a process of economic globalization which after 1989 no longer faced any obstacles)—constituted by the infrastructure of production, the organization of consumption (via psychotechnologies), and the objects and services of this consumption itself (all of which are themselves industrialized and technicized)—the becoming of this *global, technical system* tends to become *totally integrated into the economic system and submitted to its priorities as well as to its contradictions.*

In addition, the economic system is henceforth almost completely directed by the financial sub-system, itself globalized, and this financial sub-system, in turn, is itself structurally de-correlated from the production sub-system.

Technical system, social systems, and marketing

From the Napoleonic state until various forms of Keynesianism, and passing through Gaullism, one function of the state has been to ensure the direction and regulation of the disadjustment provoked by ever-more rapid evolutions of the technical system, and to implement processes of readjustment as they become necessary. Bertrand Gille wrote in 1978—one year before Thatcher came to power—that, failing such regulation, which constitutes a policy of industrial development, social systems could only find themselves annihilated by a chaotic becoming of this development.[21]

The technical system is a dynamic system in which there takes place what Simondon describes as a process of individuation. Gille shows that in the course of this individuation, the technical system enters regularly into conflict with the "other social systems"—which are themselves processes of collective individuation, and which presuppose processes of psychic individuation, and what Freud called psychic apparatuses.

This means that it is possible for the individuation of the technical system to proceed in a way that is contrary to the individuation of social systems and psychic apparatuses. This contrariness, however, *also* constitutes the dynamic of the technical, social and psychic individuation processes, that is, the pharmacological *condition* of their individuation: Simondon shows that individuation, qua process, presupposes the phase differences [*déphasages*] which precisely induce these different dynamics of individuation, and vice versa.

On the other hand, processes of *psychic and social individuation* are not in any case *adaptations* of the social systems and psychic apparatuses to the becoming of the technical system: they are processes of *adoption*, that is, of *co-individuation*, in which social systems and psychic apparatuses produce and individuate the technical system as much as they participate in their own respective individuations—and do so in a way that is transductively interlinked.

Gille argues that the state must assume the regulation of (inevitable and necessary) conflicts in order to avoid the destruction of these systems: the state regulates by determining the parameters of the technical system and the correlative evolution of the social systems through negotiation, forecasting, and planning, that is, through the long-term organization of technological and industrial becoming; it must equally ensure the possibility of research independent of private investment, which is short-termist when compared with intergenerational social time.

Such policies are therapeutics which define regimes

100

of individuation based on long circuits of transindividuation, and which prescribe conditions in which technological and industrial pharmacology produces individuation more than it does disindividuation.

Now, an essential aspect of the ideological war led by the neoliberals of the conservative revolution was the condemnation of governmental industrial and long-term policy and the corresponding accusation that governments inevitably promote inefficient models of economic administration—even though the United States military continues to determine the direction of the industrial policies of the American state. This eventually evolved into the accusation that *all* social structures that produce long circuits of transindividuation are guilty of curbing the modernization made possible by the development of the technical system.

When Thatcher and Reagan initiated deregulation, dismantling and eventually liquidating all state apparatuses, their gamble was that these adjustment processes could be entrusted to the operation of the market alone, that is, to marketing, which then exploits *without limit* the psychotechnologies constituting the media infrastructure—and does so at the service of a behavioral control which is "narcotic," that is, which is anaesthetizing and which produces addiction.

Confounding the technical and economic systems as a principal factor of carelessness

This *unlimited* exploitation leads to the slow but inexorable liquidation of the *apparatus of production of libidinal energy, an apparatus formed by conjoining psychic apparatuses and social systems so as to produce sublimation systems* (and which concretize individuation insofar as it is always at once psychic and collective). In the autumn of 2008, this unlimited exploitation will turn out to have installed a genuinely *planetary carelessness*.

The *confounding of the technical and economic systems* is a catastrophe which inevitably leads these two systems, which are thoroughly pharmacological, to potentize and exacerbate their toxic, entropic and self-destructive tendencies—for four reasons:

1. The subordination of the technical to the economic system, itself dominated by the highly speculative and short-termist financial sub-system, reinforces the destructive effects of innovation and of the acceleration of innovation for the other social systems: the technical system incessantly disadjusts from the social systems. And it tends to bury, suppress, and delay the effects of this disadjustment by substituting for these social systems technical processes amount-

ing to services which short-circuit that process of transindividuation of which these social systems are the organization—the absence of regulation leading in the end to the destruction of temporalities (long circuits) which are not immediately "monetizable," that is, capable of being absorbed by a consumer market.

2. The extremely rapid and violent penetration of technology in the different social systems (family systems, education systems, political systems, judicial systems, linguistic systems, etc.) leads to generalized proletarianization: technological innovation is imposed through marketing as a process of adaptation of psychic and social individuals, and not appropriated as a vector of individuation and process of adoption defining a therapeutic regime, that is, *savoir-vivre* (*therapeuma* and *epimeleia* as techniques of self and others). This is why it no longer allows the creation of circuits of transindividuation and on the contrary sets as its principle the short-circuiting of the transindividuation process—which amounts to a principle of *systemic carelessness*.

3. The short-termist pressure exerted by fictitious capital and shareholder management over the development of a technical system entirely subordinated to the economy and therefore to the market, and for which

the only developmental possibilities that come to be selected are those enabling the *very rapid constitution of solvencies*—thereby closing off all possibilities for social investment in the *pharmakon*, both in the long term and as therapeutic implementation of its socialization—this pressure of the economic system on the technical system leads to a systemically careless development *of the technical system itself.*

4. The geographical, biological, demographic and psychic systems find themselves disadjusted, leading to their disequilibrium, rather than to beneficial disruptions (that is, to disruptions that would be effectively negentropic, disruptions capable of leading to the production of *new metastabilities*, such as would occur if the *pharmakon* were implemented therapeutically).

The collapse of the system of motivations

Human becoming is the result of a threefold process of individuation for which the technical system, social systems and psychic apparatuses are the meta-stable configurations engendering processes of technical, collective and psychic individuation. These three individuation processes are inseparable: they form transductive relations.[22]

104

These transductive relations tie together three organological levels which must be distinguished, and which have their own logic and their own tendencies, but which cannot be considered in isolation from one another:

- The psychic apparatus is based on a system of psychosomatic organs;
- The technical system connects artificial organs which become the *pharmaka* of the psychosomatic body, connecting it to other bodies at the heart of social systems;
- Social systems are the organizations through which the transindividual metastabilizes and unifies the therapeutic regimes which constitute social blending [*faire-corps*] through the collective individuation process.

That the technical system is in transductive relation with the social systems means that it cannot be developed without a human milieu in relation to which it is exogenous, a milieu formed out of psychic and collective individuals *cultivating their singularities by cultivating consistences, that is, objects which do not exist, but which are infinite*—and which, as such, permit the unification at infinity (infinitely to come) of systems and individuals.

That the psychic apparatus is in transductive relation with the technical system means that psychic apparatuses cannot socialize without passing through the *pharmaka* constitutive of the technical system—which is also a system of tertiary retentions,[23] and which thus supports individual and collective protentions (and the formation of credit). These *pharmaka* permit the formation of both long and short transindividuation circuits.

Reciprocally, social systems, as processes of collective individuation, that is, as evolving systems, cannot perpetuate themselves without adopting *pharmaka* through the psychic individuals who transindividuate themselves at the heart of these social systems, *pharmaka* which as such disrupt the organizations in which these systems consist: each organological level being individuated in transductive relation to the individuation of the other systems.

In the twentieth century, however, the economic system having taken a step beyond all the other systems, and being charged with the task of unifying them *by finitizing them*, that is, submitting them to a process of generalized "monetization"—and the financial sub-system having taken a step beyond the production sub-system at the heart of the economic system itself—it is *infinitive consistence* (the law of desire), constituting the condition of any genuine co-individuation of the

106

three organological levels, which finds itself destroyed. Now, there can be no *sustainable* (that is, care-ful [*curieuse*]) *protention* without infinitive consistency.

This results in both the squeezing of all anticipations into an ultra-short-term horizon of speculation, and the collapse of the system of motivations. Speculation, very far from producing a new dynamic, on the contrary fossilizes time: it freezes it into a wall of time where past and future cancel each other out, and where all forms of investment disintegrate. The ultra-short-term tendency of completely deregulated fictitious capital, which systemically short-circuits the process of transindividuation, thereby causes fictitious capital to become totalized and extremist. This tendency is, then, intrinsically self-destructive and as such annihilates time—time, of which the law is *desire, insofar as it permits the realization (through sublimation) of motives of imagination (possibilities).*

Such a situation of carelessness—which can only lead to the entropic disintegration of the three organological levels, while at the same time destroying the *extra*-organological systems (geographical, climatological, geological, and biological systems)—is induced by a consumerist model which, having reached its limits through the spread of dissociated milieus,[24] that is, proletarianized milieus, becomes self-destructive, insofar as what it destroys is not merely the desire of consumers but also their health.

The reinvention of the industrial economy presupposes the reconstitution of a libidinal economy without which there can be no investment, and this means that *new apparatuses of production of libidinal energy must be conceived and instituted*—because *such apparatuses are necessarily institutions*: hence the ecclesiastical institution and its care-ful [*curieux*] inhabitant, the curé; hence the school and its master, the teacher [*instituteur*].

To economize anew, that is, *to struggle against the care-less tendency* inherent to that *pharmakon* that is capital, and *thus to take care of the world*, can clearly no longer pass by way of "stimulating consumption." But neither can it pass by way of a "decrease in growth" ["*décroissance*"]. Rather, a pathway to *genuine* growth must be refound, a growth running counter to the mis-growth [*mécroissance*] that consumerism has become,[25] and a growth which would consist in a renaissance of desire. Such a rebirth would be achieved by implementing an economy of contribution, an economy for which "*to economize*" means "*to take care*,"[26] and an economy within which care cultivates associated milieus.[27]

108

Pharmacology of technical tendencies

In the course of his ethnographic research, and by comparing ethnic groups, André Leroi-Gourhan created the concept of what he called "*technical tendencies.*" Technical tendencies emerge from that "interior milieu" which the "ethnic group" constitutes. Technical tendencies emerging from the ethnic group are projected in the form of technical objects, the totality of which constitute a "membrane" (or a "film") through which the ethnic group takes hold of its exterior milieu, which it thus assimilates via its technical objects.

Leroi-Gourhan's analysis is greatly inspired both by Henri Bergson, as Leroi-Gourhan explicitly acknowledges with his references to the theory of "life force," and by Claude Bernard, who makes use of the concepts of interior milieu, exterior milieu, as well as of membrane and cell, in order to describe the "metabolic" functions of socio-ethnic groups.

Now, the interior milieu in which technical tendencies are formed is at the same time the seat of counter-tendencies *limiting* their concrete expression. The interior milieu "secretes" these tendencies, but it *also* secretes something similar to an (auto-)immune system in order to struggle against the toxic effects that these tendencies may at times provoke within the interior milieu.

This is in effect constituted through a technical milieu which supports it, which is its condition, and which is its double (in the double sense of the word, if I may put it like this): the technical milieu (equivalent to what Bertrand Gille called the technical system), harbored by the interior milieu, and supporting it, also does not cease to exceed it and to threaten it with destruction, as though it were a parasite that also happens to be the condition of possibility (and of impossibility) of that upon which it is parasitical. In brief, it is a matter of a pharmacological milieu, bearing tendencies which are curative as well as poisonous.

This is why, within the interior milieu, a technical tendency, though it has its provenance in this milieu, is never completely expressed within that milieu: a technical tendency is only realized through technical facts which are a compromise between technical characteristics, emerging from the tendency, and ethnic characteristics that Leroi-Grouhan describes as degrees of technical fact[28] limiting this tendency—degrees of which the first is the pure tendency, but which is therefore covered over by other degrees which mask it, limiting its expression, indeed returning the technicity of the tendency against its own expression. In certain regards, there is a manifest content (which is the technical fact) and a latent content (which is the technical tendency)—the manifest content expressing the latent content only by dissimulating it, *deferring* [*différant*] it, and *differentiating* [*différenciant*] itself from it.

Such is the case because the interior milieu (which constitutes the ethnic group) harbors within the technical milieu a social sub-group (the technical group), bearer of the tendency, which is distinguished from other social groups, themselves bearers of counter-tendencies emerging from other social systems. A social counter-tendency consists in causing the technical tendency to "diffract," to deflect, and even to reverse its direction, in order to ensure that the technical tendency does not destroy those systems constituting the interior milieu, which would be inevitable were it to be expressed without any limitation whatsoever. The tendency which bears the technical group is therefore concretely expressed as a technical fact in the encounter with other social groups which take hold of this tendency in causing it to bifurcate.

This deflection, this diffraction, and the bifurcations which are produced by it, and which are specific forms of what Derrida described as *différance* (which is also an economy)[29] constitutes the reality of the process of co-individuation of the technical system with the social systems—and, through them, the individuation of the psychic systems that anticipate them and realize them just as much as they are submitted to them and find themselves conditioned by them.

In contrast with these conservative reactions of the interior milieu, however, the technical group, which tends to facilitate the expression of the technical tendency, is a step ahead when compared to the ethnic group, insofar as it is extremely aware of elements of the exterior milieu

> that we must [. . .] understand first of all as a natural milieu, which is inert, composed of stones, wind, trees, and animals, but also as the bearer of the objects and the ideas of different human groups.[30]

The technical group is, then, what causes the passing into action (or the transgression [*passer à l'acte*]) of the technical tendency (which is nothing other than a potential), via the intermediary of objects and ideas coming from the exterior milieu, that technicians assimilate, and through which they take a step ahead of the interior milieu. The interior group is, however, led to itself assimilate this technical milieu in order to be able to assimilate that which, in its exterior milieu, has changed, something Leroi-Gourhan demonstrates with his example of the snowshoe, adopted by the Alaskan Inuit because their climate was becoming frozen: everything here is a matter of arrangements between dynamic systems.

The economy of contribution as the overturning [renversement] of the bearish macro-tendency

The technical tendencies proper to human groups[31] define the human as such, and threaten the human as such: they threaten the cohesive factors unifying the group. Technical tendencies originate from the ethnic group itself. Leroi-Gourhan's "technical milieu" may be a step ahead when compared with the interior milieu, yet it is so, if one can put it like this, from out of this interior and, in some way, by *hollowing out* this interior. In Gille's account, on the other hand, the technical system and its dynamic seem to become exteriorized, to detach from the interior milieu, and to de-correlate from the social systems: this is what Gille describes as disadjustment.

The societies of which Gille speaks are no longer ethnic and tribal groups: they are much larger social groups (empires, politically and economically organ-ized and hierarchized cities, churches, nations, etc.), the social structures of which are profoundly distant from those of ethnic groups, as well as being divided and differentiated into sub-groups, social classes, economic sectors, etc.

In these hierarchical societies, social groups are in a relation to other social groups with which they form a unity (imperial, political, religious, national, etc.), as if these "ethnic cells" have integrated to form a superior body constituting a new interior milieu. Furthermore, such hierarchical societies maintain commercial and military relations with one another, leading to an exterior milieu that is more and more strongly "anthropized," that is, technicized: a milieu of exchanges and of "external commerce," through which international law can form, which is sometimes an economic site, and at other times a site of war.

Disadjustment is manifested in the spatial differentiation which urbanization induces. But it has only become a perceptible and constant factor of the social dynamic since the time of the industrial revolution. The technical system then tends to blanket and absorb the social systems, first of all by inscribing *savoir-faire* into machines (by grammatizing knowledge), then by short-circuiting *savoir-vivre* via the apparatus supporting the service industries (in the consumerist epoch), contemporary reticulated society grammatizing social relations themselves via *social engineering*.

There have always been, in all preceding periods of

human society, processes de-correlating the technical system from the social systems, and the technical milieu has always exceeded the interior milieu—something the Greeks characterized as a form of *hubris*. But for the past ten thousand years of sedentary life and urbanized civilization, such processes—which disrupt the social system and the overall collective individuation process, and which are provoked by "leaps" in the individuation of the technical system—always constituted exceptional episodes.

Disadjustment becomes chronic from the time of the industrial revolution. And this becomes even more the case at the beginning of the twentieth century, when industry, struggling against the tendential decline in the rate of profit, systematically organizes a form of permanent innovation which presupposes the development of a consumerist society, and which depends upon the systematic and continual transformation of ways of life.

From that point, not only does the technical system no longer seem to be secreted by the ethnic group—a situation which began from the moment the ethnic "cell" became integrated with other, similar "cells" in order to form a more complex social body—but it seems as though the technical system, in fact, escapes to a new interior milieu within this complex body. Such is the process of *dissociation*, a process through which social systems cease to appropriate the technical tendency by deflecting it and individuating it, but rather in which the social systems themselves are short-circuited and literally dis-integrated via the technicization of the social.

Within this process, the economic system too is de-correlated from the other social systems, both through financialization and by taking control of the technical system, which thus becomes the vector of deterritorialization. The technical tendencies no longer proceed from out of the interior milieu, and are no longer secreted by it, to the extent that *there no longer is an interior milieu*: the technical milieu, passing into the control of a technical system itself largely deterritorialized and globalized, leads to the pure and simple dilution of the interior milieu, as if it had been parasitized—and poisoned.

This amounts, then, to the attaining of a limit—because the dilution of interior milieus is also the disintegration of psychic apparatuses, as well as the total exhaustion of libidinal energy and of capacities for investment, anticipation, and will. According to the principles of general organology, a technical milieu stripped of the interior milieu is a process of technical individuation stripped of the process of psychosocial individuation, and is hence a process which inevitably becomes entropic, given that it has destroyed its energy base—libidinal energy, which is a necessary condition for every kind of protention—and given that technical tendencies are actualized in technical facts which are the material expression of these tendencies.

Having reached this stage, the tendential decline in the rate of profit, and its consumerist and speculative counter-tendency, together engender a bearish macro-tendency which eventually becomes unsustainable: such is our lot. In order to *overturn this tendency*, it is essential [*capital*] to reconstitute a process of individuation of the technical milieu through the individuation of a new type of interior milieu (constituted by "multitudes" of "cells") via investment in the relational technologies characteristic of reticulated societies.

The therapeutic program of this pharmacology, which rests on the formation of new associated milieus, is the economy of contribution.[32]

Organology of tendencies and of their transductive arrangements

There are tendencies and counter-tendencies proper to each of the three organological levels, but these arrange and tie together the transductive relations between the three levels:

- At the psychosomatic level, drive-based and sublimatory tendencies and counter-tendencies play out, the compromise between which constitutes a libidinal economy—expressed concretely in the course of time through psychic configurations which are each time specific—by arranging pharmacological possibilities and through being projected across *pharmaka* on the social plane, where psychic individuation equally becomes collective individuation and the formation of a circuit of transindividuation;

- At the technical and pharmacological level, technical tendencies play out, which are only expressed concretely as technical facts encountering counter-tendencies elicited by other social systems, which thus cross, animate, structure and individuate the technical system itself—an encounter which always takes place through psychic individuals inscribing their psychic individuation within collective individuation;

- At the social level, which is that of organizations and institutions of collective individuation, tendencies metastabilizing toward synchronization (where synchronization is the condition of unity of the social level in its totality) play both with and against diachronizing tendencies, which incessantly jostle against these structures which are metastabilized through collective individuation—under the impetus

118

of psychic individuals themselves individuated and diachronically singularized through their relation to *pharmaka* (and to technical tendencies), wherever therapeutic spaces deriving from the social level make this possible.

It is through these arrangements of multilayered tendencies that transindividuation processes are woven. Each of the social systems is itself constituted by specific tendencies which instantiate the dynamics of synchronization and diachronization, and which form its own circuits of transindividuation.

Nevertheless, with each new stage of grammatization, new synchronization processes, that is, new regimes of metastabilization, are enabled. But beginning with that grammatization process which enabled the discretization of corporeal flows, in turn enabling their calculation via machine tools and the apparatus of production, management and conception, and eventually via the psychotechnologies orchestrating consumption (making it possible to calculate the flux of consciousness—"available brain-time"), the economic system takes a step beyond all the other social systems by taking control of the technical system itself—that is, by controlling which possibilities are selected from amongst all those constituting the protentional fields opened up by technical tendencies, and by imposing favorable technical facts on fictitious capital, which is itself imposed on productive capital.

Grammatization—that is, pharmacology—is nevertheless what also enables new processes of diachronization—that is, of individuation. Faced with the bearish macro-tendency described in the preceding paragraphs, a macro-tendency amounting to a negative arrangement of tendencies issuing from the three organological levels, we must reactivate an inherent *tendency toward elevation* in human societies, and which was translated, at a certain stage of grammatization, and via the hypomnesic *pharmakon*, into the culture of consistences of the *skhole* and *otium*.

The tendency to elevation—"there are a lot of alternatives"

For every stage of grammatization, societies institute therapeutic systems, systems of care, techniques of self and others, which constitute spiritualities and diverse noetic forms, from shamanistic models to artistic models, passing through churches, medical therapies, schools, sports, philosophies, and every system of sublimation.

These systems, which are concrete expressions of the tendency to cultivate consistences, nevertheless presuppose the apparatus of production of subsistences with which they compose, and through which is formed a *negotium* which, as commerce, is also a calculation about what does exist and what will exist. What composes together, then, is the *otium* of consistences, the *negotium* of subsistences and that which constitutes existences worthy of this name—through which a *savoir-vivre* is formed that one can call *existence*.

The economy of contribution is the stimulation of desire through the reconstitution of systems of care founded on contemporary *pharmaka* and constituting a new commerce of subsistences in the service of a new existence.

In the course of history, human societies arrange, combine, and economize various tendencies and counter-tendencies which weave and metastabilize the dynamic systems that are formed on the three organological levels. These arrangements are formed by potentizing [*potentialisant*] the tendencies and counter-tendencies occurring at these three levels. The dynamic historical processes resulting from these arrangements are generated from out of the limits of those which precede them, and they are subsequently transformed through the encounter with their own limits. We live at such a moment—to a very grave degree: to the degree that the very survival of humankind is at stake.

Toward the end of the twentieth century, the tendential fall in the rate of profit, counteracted by counter-tendencies harnessing libidinal energy, in the end produced *a conjunction of the drive-based tendency of the psychic system and the speculative tendency of the economic system*. But in the new pharmacological context created by digital networks, *a contrary arrangement* clearly becomes imaginable: one can imagine that *tendencies to investment* could be combined with *sublimatory tendencies*.

These arrangements presuppose articulations between the economic system and the psychic apparatus at both the organizational level and the psychosomatic level. These articulations are translated at the level of the technical system by giving orientations to technical tendencies, and more precisely through the types of technical fact which are then selected by the economic system conjoined to the psychic system, technical facts which concretely express technical tendencies: the technical tendency that comes to be expressed in a technical system is not a determination, no more than the tendential fall in the rate of profit determines the end of capitalism—and the technical reality is not the tendency, but the fact. On the other hand, the tendency opens various possibilities, and that is why to the TINA ideology, "*there is no alternative*," one must oppose the TALOA argument, "*there are lots of alternatives*."

Tendencies are potentials lying within the interior and from which possibilities can be selected: they open fields of protentional possibilities. Possibilities which are selected are then expressed concretely as technical facts, but these are always oriented through social systems. Social systems, on the other hand, are themselves currently involved in a struggle for control of collective individuation. Our epoch is characterized by the fact that it is the economic system dominated by fictitious capital that imposes a technical system the evolutions of which it presents as ineluctable—an ineluctability supposedly extending to the liquidation not only of the state, but of all long circuits of transindividuation, which was the very thing advocated by Thatcher and Reagan in the 1980s, and still advocated by Sarkozy and Berlusconi in the 2000s. But in reality such arrangements are historical, and perfectly contingent—what is more, they are profoundly toxic.

From drive-based emptiness to the overturning of the tendency

The ultraliberal parameters of the technical system which led to what proved to be the catastrophe of 2008 were directed solely by the short term, that is, by technical facts organized and produced through marketing—a marketing which denies that long-term tendencies exist: nothing other than the market can direct becoming, we are informed by this "managerial dogmatism,"[33] and it is just too bad if this becoming [*devenir*] turns out to no longer have any future [*avenir*].

Those arguing for and explicitly demanding this denial of long-term existence, and finally of time itself (that is, of the individuation of singularities, of existence), claim that it is not possible to predict the technical future, nor is it possible to build any kind of political will or bring it into reality. But this devaluing of anticipation, which in its own terms is contradictory to *all* forms of investment, rests on a confusion operating between technical fact and technical tendency.

Leroi-Gourhan in effect shows that it is entirely possible to anticipate technical becoming, on the condition that we understand that becoming, oriented, encouraged and moved by technical tendencies, is "diffracted" and deflected into technical facts which, in the short

124

term, can seem perfectly clearly to totally contradict this tendency (just as the current of a river, observed at a very reduced scale, can give the feeling of flowing from east to west whereas it is in fact flowing from west to east, because the observed portion, being a whirlpool, engenders contrary currents), indeed to durably block it (an available technique can be utilized in order to counteract the new technique of which the tendency is a bearer).

Such apparent contradictions are possible because technical facts are compromises between technical tendencies and social systems, which are themselves organizations resulting from tendencies and counter-tendencies constituting them as metastable systems.[34] The question then becomes to know how a public power can, without reducing all social systems to the economic system (because this would be to dissolve desire into pure calculability), create adjustments enabling the reconstruction of the long term, anticipation, investment, etc.

The careless tendency substituting the market for commerce is currently dominant, a tendency resulting from a *toxic combination of tendencies and counter-tendencies* at the three organological levels. This toxic economy of regressive tendencies, implemented by consumerism exercising the psychopower of its cultural hegemony through the intermediary of psychotechnologies, in this way controls the becoming of individual and collective behavior, as well as the dynamic processes of the technical system. From the resulting destruction of circuits of transindividuation also results the dilution of those interior milieus constituting human groups.

"Internalizing" ["*intérioriser*"] capitalism and its functioning, if one still wishes to speak the language of Boltanski and Chiapello, presupposes that the interior milieu has not been completely diluted—failing which, there is no longer any internalization, but only pure exteriorization leading to a drive-based emptiness. Such are the systemically bearish consequences—consequences which include the production of an immense systemic stupidity[35]—of the tendential fall in the rate of profit and its consumerist counter-tendency.

The tendency to carelessness is irreducible: there is not, there never has been and there never will be a paradise on earth. This is why it is necessary to organize an economy of carelessness by cultivating systems of care which presuppose a pharmacological intelligence, concretely expressing in this way an art of living, weaving therapeutic multiples. Our epoch is, however, very singular: unlike any other before it, *it has made carelessness into the very principle of its organization*. This is what can no longer be endured.

126

Such are the urgency and the challenge—global and unprecedented—to conduct a grand overturning of tendencies in the face of generalized drive-based emptiness.

The economy of contribution as a new relation between the technical system and social systems

Under the influence of technical tendencies, the becoming of the technical system—in particular after the advent of industrialization, and through those very specific technical objects that are machines, then apparatus—is traversed by a process of concretization which is realized through the integration of functions, a process through which several functions come to be founded on a single function, which thus becomes plurifunctional.

Gilbert Simondon analyzes this process of becoming in particular in relation to heat engines: his first example is the passage from external combustion (the furnace), which moves the piston of the steam engine, to the combustion produced in the interior of the cylinder, where the piston slides open due to the force of the explosion of a gas, a passage which occurs when the Lenoir engine replaces the steam engine in the series of heat engines.[36]

Another case of functional integration appears with

what Simondon calls the techno-geographic milieu associated with the functioning of a technical system. Simondon developed this theory in relation to the Guimbal turbine, for which he showed that the marine element is functionally integrated into the engine and thus becomes an associated techno-geographical milieu. Other forms of techno-geographical milieu exist, not strictly associated with the technical system, but adapted via a technique which forms an intermediary between it and the geographical milieu, and which as such forms a techno-geographical milieu. Consider, for example, the contours of a stretch of land, worked upon and technicized so that it can incorporate a rail network, and enabling a locomotive to be adapted to these contours of land: in this situation, the network constitutes an interface between the geographical system and the technical system.

In 1990 Philippe Aigrin and myself put forward the idea that the software industry and its digital networks will eventually cause associated techno-geographical milieus of a new kind to appear, enabling human geography to interface with the technical system, to make it function and, especially, make it evolve, thanks to this interfacing:[37] collaborative technologies and free license software rest precisely on the valorization of such associated human milieus, which also constitute techno-geographical spaces for the formation of positive externalities.

This process is an inter-systemic macro-tendency formed at the interface of the technical system and social systems, and operating a functional integration between them—but where this integration is, however, not necessarily beneficial: it is highly pharmacological, and hence, for example, social networks are clearly also connected to processes of automated traceability, set into motion by actions and requests that network actors mostly produce without even knowing it, but which confer to those who obtain this information a new type of power.

Here, the interface between the technical system and social systems does not operate via the economic system, but precisely through those social systems which are bearers of the knowledge [*savoirs*] which society holds. Such forms of knowledge and their valorization are the only possibilities we have for struggling against the production of information *without* knowledge. Developing such forms of knowledge and valuing them economically will cause a new economic system to emerge from the heart of the social systems, and respecting these social systems means constituting an economy of contribution, *contra* the economy of carelessness.

For a New Critique of Political Economy

Introduction

1 These concepts are developed in *La Technique et le Temps 3: Le temps du cinéma et la question du mal-être* (Paris: Galilée, 2001). A summary can be found in *Philosopher par accident*, with Elie During (Paris: Galilée, 2004), pp. 74ff.

2 *La Technique et le Temps 3*.

Pharmacology of the proletariat

1 A podcast is available on the Ars Industrialis website: http://www.arsindustrialis.org

2 http://www.ccic-cerisy.asso.fr/activitemarchande08.html

3 Christian Fauré, Alain Giffard, Bernard Stiegler, *Pour en finir avec la mécroissance. Quelques propositions d'Ars Industrialis* (Paris: Flammarion, 2009).

4 In particular André Gorz.

5 And this would be contrary to the fantasy, inspired by incautious readings of Hannah Arendt, that seeks to *purify* "the political" of anything economic.

6 See Jeremy Rifkin, *The End of Work: The Decline of the Global Labor Force and the Dawn of the Post-Market Era* (New York: Putnam Books, 1995). And Michel Rocard, "Preface," to Rifkin, *La Fin du travail*, trans. P. Rouve (Paris: La Découverte, 2006).

130

7 Dominique Méda, *Le Travail. Une valeur en voie de disparition* (Paris: Aubier, 1995).

8 André Gorz, *Métamorphoses du travail. Critique de la raison économique* (Paris: Gallimard, 2004). In English, *Critique of Economic Reason*, trans. C. Turner and G. Handyside (London: Verso, 1989).

9 Antonella Corsani and Maurizio Lazzarato, *Intermittents et précaires* (Paris: Amsterdam, 2008).

10 McKenzie Wark, *A Hacker Manifesto* (Cambridge, Massachusetts: Harvard University Press, 2004).

11 Pekka Himanen, *The Hacker Ethic: A Radical Approach to the Philosophy of Business* (New York: Random House, 2002).

12 The new question of work is also that of a new attitude, which is characteristic of the aspirations of younger generations. I argued in *La Télécratie contre la démocratie* (Paris: Flammarion, 2006) that the demonstrations of French students against the CPE (Contrat Premier Emploi: a first job contract) were before anything else a protest against the confusion between work and job: "Not all employment is work: not all jobs are conducive to the acquisition and development of knowledge and therewith, to individuation, that is, the process whereby you can make a place for yourself in society as a producer, *and not only as a consumer whose job furnishes the employee a salary which in turn confers buying power.* Individuation is on the contrary *what takes work beyond mere employment,* if one understands that 'work' *consists in action in the world in order to transform it on the basis of the knowledge one has of it.* Now work, to the extent that it has been affected by grammatization, in the secondary as well as in the tertiary sectors, insofar as it has become more and more a matter of 'wages,' is today most often reduced to the time spent in employment: this is what results from the

spread of dissociated milieus, a spread which is itself the first consequence of the grammatization of gestures and modes of production in which the industrial revolution consists" (*Télécratie contre la démocratie*, pp. 243–4). I will return to these questions in more detail further on.

13 It is this "at once" that Immanuel Wallerstein has perhaps overlooked in his reference to the theory of cycles.

14 I try to describe the negative dynamic of this exhaustion in *Pour en finir avec la mécroissance*.

15 That is to say, the increase in the fixed capital component (the means of production) and the corresponding decrease of variable capital (wage labor) which Marx shows to be the result of a decrease in the profitability of investment.

16 Bernard Stiegler, *Économie de l'hypermatériel et du psychopouvoir. Entretiens avec Philippe Petit et Vincent Bontens* (Paris: Mille et une nuits, 2008).

17 *Pour en finir avec la mécroissance*.

18 Jeremy Rifkin, *The Age of Access: The New Culture of Hypercapitalism Where All of Life Is a Paid-for Experience* (New York: Putnam, 2000), p. 9.

19 Karl Marx, *Contribution to a Critique of Political Economy*, trans. S. W. Ryanzanskaya (Moscow: Progress Publishers, 1970), pp. 195–6.

20 *Ibid.*, p. 197.

21 Guy Debord, *The Society of the Spectacle*, trans. Donald Nicholson-Smith (New York: Zone Books, 1995), p. 159.

22 Jacques Derrida, *Dissemination*, trans. Barbara Johnson (Chicago: Chicago University Press, 1981), pp. 61–171.

23 Gilles Deleuze and Félix Guattari, *Anti-Oedipus*, trans. Robert Hurley, Mark Seem, and Helen R. Lane (Minneapolis: University of Minnesota Press, 1983), pp. 144–5.

24 "[A] memory of words (*paroles*) and no longer a memory of

things, a memory of signs and no longer of effects." *Anti-Oedipus*, p. 144.

25 Scott Lash and Celia Lury, *Global Culture Industry* (London: Polity, 2007).

26 The reader may consult the report of the International Telecommunication Union: http://www.itu.int/itunews/manager/display.asp?lang=en&year=2005&issue=09&ipage=things&ext=html

27 Grammatization is the condition of possibility of what Guy Debord calls materialized ideology. See *The Society of the Spectacle*, pp. 212–13. But Debord does not think grammatization itself, nor its pharmacological character, and this constitutes a blockage in his thought.

28 *Mécréance et discrédit 3. L'esprit perdu du capitalisme* (Paris: Galilée, 2006).

29 Karl Marx and Friedrich Engels, *The Communist Manifesto*, trans. Samuel Moore (London: Penguin Books, 1967), p. 88.

30 *Ibid.*

31 Jacques Rancière, *The Nights of Labor: The Workers' Dream in 19th Century France*, trans. John Drury (Philadelphia: Temple University Press, 1989).

32 *Hypomnemata* are mnemo-techniques, which is also to say hypomnesic *pharmaka*, shown by Michel Foucault to play a decisive role in the formation of *otium* and more widely in the processes of sublimation that he describes as "techniques of the self." On these questions, see *Mécréance et discrédit 1. La decadence des démocraties industrielles* (Paris: Galilée, 2004), p. 107 forthcoming in English translation from Polity, and Stiegler and Ars Industrialis, *Réenchanter le monde: La valeur esprit contre le populisme industriel* (Paris: Flammarion, 2006) p. 31 forthcoming in English translation from Continuum.

33 Paul-Laurent Assoun, *Le Fétichisme* (Paris: PUF, 2006).

34 Bakhtin's dialogical theory is close to the Simondonian conception of linguistic individuation: no psycholinguistic individuation can take place without also consisting in a socio-linguistic individuation.

35 *Mécréance et discrédit 1*, p. 76 and p. 88.

36 One speaks of "diseconomy" in order to qualify the destructive dynamic brought about by negative externalities, that is, by environmental disorders whose costs are not paid by economic actors but which nevertheless fragilize the general economy.

37 These social networks based on the web 2.0 are produced by social engineering and by developments in what is called the social web, the most famous instance of which is Facebook, which in August 2008 passed 160 million members. There are, however, all sorts of other dimensions to these digital "relational technologies." The second of the *Entretiens du nouveau monde industriel*, organized by *Cap Digital*, the *École supérieure de creation industrielle*, and the Pompidou Center's *Institut de recherche et d'innovation*, will be on this subject, forthcoming from Mille et une nuits.

38 Several studies have highlighted this, one in particular devoted to the effects of television and DVD on children under three years of age, a study headed by Frederic Zimmerman and Dimitri Christakis at the University of Washington. On this subject, see Stiegler, *Taking Care of Youth and the Generations*, trans. Stephen Barker (Stanford: Stanford University Press, 2010), p. 56.

To work

 1 Maurizio Lazzarato shows very well how this *elimination of the time of knowledge* constitutes the very heart of the project of a "government of inequalities" in which neoliberalism

essentially consists, and it does so at the very moment when an ideology abounds which would have us believe that the very cognitive capitalism responsible for proletarianizing the "knowers" ["*sachants*"], as Jean-François Lyotard called them, could in fact be made to pass for a "knowledge society." See Lazzarato, *Le Gouvernement des inégalités, Critique de l'insécurité néolibérale* (Paris: Amsterdam, 2008).

2 *Mécréance et discrédit 1*, p. 120.

3 Maurizio Lazzarato, *Puissance de l'innovation. La psychologie économique de Gabriel Tarde contre l'economie politique* (Paris: Les Empêcheurs de tourner en rond, 2002) and *Le Gouvernment des inégalités*. In the analyses proposed in 2002, Lazzarato, who refers to Gabriel de Tarde, singularly neglects the question of hypomnesis without which such cooperation would be impossible, and, along with hypomnesis, he overlooks the retentional systems that enable the control of this cooperation, as well as the proletarianization of the activity of brains themselves, both on the side of production and on that of consumption. On the other hand, in 2008, he describes the effects of this proletarianization and the system of the management of inequalities with a view, not to cooperation between brains, but to competition between nervous systems for access, not to work, but merely to employment.

4 Yann Moulier-Boutang, himself citing Lazzarato, sets out his theses in *Le Capitalisme cognitif. La nouvelle grande transformation* (Paris: Amsterdam, 2007).

5 Himanen, *The Hacker Ethic*.

6 Wark, *A Hacker Manifesto*.

7 Moulier-Boutang, *Le Capitalisme cognitif*, pp. 199ff.

8 On this question, see Faure, Giffard and Stiegler, *Pour en finir avec la mécroissance*.

9 This dialogism is less that of dialectics than the dialogism

of Bakhtin. See *La Télécratie contre la démocratie* and *Réenchanter le monde.*

10 "*Économiser signifie prendre soin*" ["Economizing means taking care"] is the title of a seminar I gave in the spring of 2008 at the *Collège International de philosophie* as a part of the theoretical activities of Ars Industrialis. An audio recording is available at www.arsindustrialis.org

11 Corsani and Lazzarato, *Intermittents et précaires*, p. 121.

12 *Ibid.* p. 121.

13 Rifkin, *The End of Work*, "Introduction."

14 Jean-Marie André, *L'otium dans la vie morale et intellectualle romaine des origines à l'époque augustéenne* (Paris: PUF, 1965), p. 177.

15 In *Mécréance et discrédit 1* I argue that the noetic soul passes into the noetic act only intermittently, and therefore lives as *being-only-in-intermittence.*

16 Corsani and Lazzarato, *Intermittents et précaires*, p. 122.

17 Lazzarato, *Le Gouvernement des inégalités*, p. 43.

18 Michel Rocard, "Preface" to Rifkin, *La Fin du travail.*

19 On these concepts, see *La Télécratie contre la démocratie.*

20 These two economic and historical realities are very different, even though Lazzarato often conflates them (see especially, pp. 42–7), as many do today. Fordism has nothing to do with regulation or redistribution, and it proposed no "social property": it functionally integrates production and consummation and thereby invents consumerism. Keynesianism, on the other hand, represents a compromise between capital and labor. That these two transformations of the relation between capital and labor can be combined is clear enough, but from that it does not follow that they should be conflated: on the contrary, it is necessary to distinguish them in order to understand how they can be combined and, finally, how they can decompose.

21 The denial of the epistemological scope of psychoanalysis by Soviet psychology and, more broadly, by Stalinist Marxists throughout the world, is intrinsically tied to this question. This is the context in which a reader of *La Nouvelle Critique*, in April 1968, asks the editors: "Would it be possible for *La Nouvelle Critique* to stage a debate between Marxists and psychoanalysts? [. . .] Young communist psychiatrists cannot understand the positions of their Soviet comrades who totally condemn this important aspect of psychiatry. A Marxist analysis of this situation is lacking" (*La Nouvelle Critique*, no. 13).

22 I have analyzed this demotivation in *Constituer l'Europe 2. Le motif européen* (Paris: Galilée, 2005), pp. 29ff.

23 The analysis of Lazzarato is here singularly clear, see in particular pp. 30–1 of *Le Gouvernement des inégalités*.

24 Gustave Flaubert, *L'Éducation sentimentale*.

25 Roland Barthes, "Musica Practica," in *Image, Music, Text* (London: Fontana, 1977), p. 149.

26 See *De la misère symbolique 2. La catastrophe du sensible* (Paris: Galilée, 2005), p. 26.

27 See *Taking Care of Youth and the Generations*.

28 Jean-Claude Milner, *Le Salaire de l'idéal. La théorie des classes et de la culture au XXième siècle* (Paris: Le Seuil, 1997).

29 *Mécréance et discrédit 1*.

30 If money is a form of grammatization and of tertiary retention, one essential question is to gauge the consequences of changes in its retentional materiality, as for example when the metal coins first introduced by the Lydians are eventually replaced by John Law's paper money, and in turn by the French Revolution's *assignats*. This is one of the important stakes of Jean Michel Rey's *Le Temps du crédit* (Paris: Desclée de Brouwer, 2002).

31 On this question, see Jean-François Lyotard, *The Inhuman:*

Reflections on Time, trans. Geoffrey Bennington and Rachel Bowlby (Cambridge: Polity, 1991).

32 Here a new reading of Lyotard's *The Postmodern Condition* would be useful: trans. Geoff Bennington and Brian Massumi (Manchester: Manchester University Press, 1992).

Pharmacology of Capital and Economy of Contribution

1 Jean-François Lyotard, *Libidinal Economy* (Bloomington and Indianapolis: Indiana University Press, 1993).
2 Ars Industrialis, an international association for an industrial politics of technologies of spirit: http://www.arsindustrialis. org
3 This conference is accessible at: http://www.arsindustrialis. org/pour-une-économie-de-la-contribution-1
4 See pp. 66 and 84.
5 In the sense in which I take this term, see p. 29ff.
6 The tendency of fictitious capital is always to reduce the rules to a minimum, if not to eliminate them altogether, in order, as frequently as possible, to unleash power.
7 See p. 41.
8 I first approached this theme of "*incurie*," in the first instance by citing Jacques Bénigne Bossuet, in *Mécréance et discrédit 1. La décadence des démocraties industrielles* (Paris: Galilée, 2004), p. 15, forthcoming in English translation from Polity Press. Proust also made use of this word in his work, *Sur la lecture* (Paris: Acte Sud, 1988), p. 34. I must thank Alain Giffard for this reference.
9 This was expressed clearly by Paul Mazur, a business partner of Edward Bernays, cited by Al Gore in *The Assault on Reason*

(New York: Penguin, 2007), p. 94. Mazur declared: "We must shift America from a needs to desire culture. [...] People must be trained to desire, to want new things, even before the old have been entirely consumed."

10 That is, of rupture with what Al Gore described as attachment in referring to the theory of John Bowlby. See Al Gore, *The Assault on Reason*.

11 Boltanski and Chiapello analyze the consequences this flexibility has for conjugal life.

12 I have tried to show how this destruction occurs in *Taking Care of Youth and the Generations,* trans. Stephen Barker (Stanford: Stanford University Press, 2010).

13 On this subject, see: Frederick J. Zimmermann, Dimitri A. Christakis and Andrew N. Meltzoff, "Television and DVD/Video Viewing in Children Younger Than 2 Years," *Archives of Pediatrics and Adolescent Medicine* 161 (2007), pp. 473–9; and Dimitri A. Christakis, Frederick J. Zimmerman et al., "Early Television Exposure and Subsequent Attentional Problems in Children," *Pedriatrics* 113 (2004), pp. 708–13.

14 See pp. 37, 48ff. and 59.

15 Luc Boltanski and Eve Chiapello, *The New Spirit of Capitalism*, trans. Gregory Elliott (New York and London: Verso, 2005), p. 10. I have tried to show in *Mécréance et discrédit 3. L'ésprit perdu du capitalisme* (Paris: Galilée, 2006) why Boltanski and Chiapello fail to grasp desire as such an economy, and why they at the same time fail to describe the consumerist libidinal economy and the impasses to which it leads. In particular, they fail to analyze the effects of the liquidation of the apparatus of production of libidinal energy, and more generally of the psychic apparatus in its links to the social and symbolic apparatus, hence their description of the flexibility of affective relations lacks consequence.

16 It is because the libidinal economy is protentional and because capital is an organization of the production of protentions that capitalism is an epoch of libidinal economy.

17 Max Weber, *The Protestant Ethic and the Spirit of Capitalism* (London: Unwin, 1930), p. 71.

18 This is what Philippe Béraud and Franck Cormerais try to think under the name, "*societal value*" ["valeur sociétale"], to which Cormerais joins the question of *societal innovation*.

19 This point is developed further in *Mécréance et discrédit 1*, pp. 95–107 and 120–4.

20 The wave of suicide committed by employees of France-Télécom is the tragic reality of the joint destruction of the apparatus of innovation and production, as well as of psychic individuals, without whom there is nothing.

21 Bertrand Gille, *Histoire des techniques* (Paris: Gallimard, 1978), p. 77: "It is no longer a matter of undergoing uncertain technological progress in its realizations, [...] of accepting willy-nilly what occurs in the technical domain and of effecting after a fashion the necessary adaptations. In all domains, in the economic as well as the military domain, the future must be organized."

22 The transductive relation is a concept elaborated by Gilbert Simondon. In a transductive relation, the terms of the relation are constituted through the relation, and do not precede the relation.

23 See p. 140.

24 See p. 37.

25 On "*mécroissance*," see Christian Fauré, Alain Giffard and Bernard Stiegler, *Pour en finir avec la mécroissance* (Paris: Flammarion, 2009), pp. 20–1.

26 On this subject, see the Ars Industrialis seminar, "*Trouver de nouvelles armes*": http://www.arsindustrialis.org/

le-séminaire-trouver-de-nouvelles-armes-collège-internatio-nal-de-philosophie

27 See p. 37 and Bernard Stiegler and Ars Industrialis, *Réenchanter le monde: La valeur esprit contre le populisme industriel* (Paris: Flammarion, 2006), pp. 49–55 forthcoming in English translation from Continuum.

28 See André Leroi-Gourhan, *Milieu et techniques* (Paris: Albin Michel, 1945).

29 See Jacques Derrida, "Différance," *Margins of Philosophy* (Chicago: University of Chicago, 1972).

30 Leroi-Gourhan, *Milieu et techniques*, p. 334.

31 These tendencies are the result of the play of two forces: physical forces and biological forces. On this subject, see Stiegler, *Technics and Time, 1: The Fault of Epimetheus*, trans. George Collins and Richard Beardsworth (Stanford: Stanford University Press, 1998). These tendencies are expressed across all human groups and in this sense they are universal. All groups harbor them, but each group concretizes them in their own way, specifically, that is, by individuating them in a specific way, and by individuating themselves through them.

32 This economy must be introduced because, before any other reason, the model of centralized networks—of telecommunication through the telephonic center, of distribution of energy through the electricity center, of production and distribution through buying centres according to the model of consumption—has been reconfigured and has given way to contributive networks, in very many domains, and for reasons of pure rationality. As far as the economy of energy is concerned, for example, centralist models have become unsustainable: energy economies are now becoming bidirectional networks, just as Jeremy Rifkin predicted, as the

contributive production of energy begins to be introduced, making possible new infrastructures—logical as well as reticulated—infrastructures that are sometimes called *smart grids*.

33 This notion of "managerial dogmatism" comes from Pierre Legendre, in *Dominium Mundi, L'empire du management* (Paris: Mille et une nuits, 2007).

34 A metastable system is a dynamic system at the limit of equilibrium and disequilibrium, and Gilbert Simondon shows that a process of individuation constitutes a dynamic system regulated through such a metastability. See Gilbert Simondon, *L'Individuation psychique et collective* (Paris: Aubier, 2007), forthcoming in English translation from University of Minnesota Press.

35 See p. 45.

36 See Gilbert Simondon, *Du mode d'existence des objets techniques* (Paris: Aubier, 1989), pp. 20–3, forthcoming in English translation from University of Minnesota Press.

37 We worked then with Alain Giffard and for the development association of the Bibliothèque Nationale de France, with a view to developing "posts for reading assisted by computer."